# PROSPECT

# PRESENTATION

# CLOSE

**YOUR THREE KEYS**
TO SUCCESSFUL SALES

## JERRY X SHEA

### AUTHOR OF:
*IT LOOKS EASY! IS IT? Simple Steps for Small Business Success.*

**ICON HOLDINGS, INC.**
Cambria · California

## WARNING-DISCLAIMER

The purpose of this book is to educate and entertain.  The author
and Icon Holdings, Inc. shall have neither liability nor responsibility
to any person or entity with respect to any loss or damage caused,
or alleged to be caused, directly or indirectly, by the information
contained in this book.

If you do not wish to be bound by the above, you may return this
book to the publisher for a full refund.

**Published by:**
>        Icon Holdings, Inc.  P.O. Box 1445, Cambria, CA 93428

# www.jerryxshea.com

**Library of Congress Catalog Card Number** 2010914798
Shea, Jerry X  1943 -
Prospecting – Presentation - Close : Your Three Keys To
Successful Sales / Jerry X Shea – 1st ed.

ISNB  978-0-9712622-1-8     Paperback
1. Small Business  2. Sales
        I. Shea, Jerry X   II. Title


Printed in the United States of America (USA) First Edition

This book is dedicated to *you*, the reader. I have put my most requested workshop into book form for *you* to learn and understand just what it takes to increase your sales efforts.

# WARNING-DISCLAIMER

_Prospecting - Presentation - Close_ is factually accurate, except that, in some cases, the names, locales, and individual traits have been fictionalized to preserve coherence while protecting privacy.

# Table of Contents

# INTRODUCTION

There is only one reason that any business goes *out-of-business --- lack of sales*. It is that simple. When a business cannot create enough sales (income) to cover all of its operating expenses, it cannot pay the bills. When that happens there are only two things you can do: increase your sales volume so that more money comes into the business to cover your expenses or inject additional money into the business via a loan or your personal savings. If business picks up as a result of your continued marketing and sales efforts, you will continue to grow your business. If, however, after you inject more money into your company you still can't increase your sales, that additional money ends up following bad money and you go *out-of-business* later than sooner.

There is no need, however, to go *out-of-business* if you can just learn to implement what it takes to increase sales. Over the years I have seen many small businesses save themselves by increasing their sales efforts. How did they do it? They reached out to new markets. At the same time I have seen many small businesses go *out-of-business* due to their inability to find new markets. It is hard to watch a nice couple put everything they have into their business only to end up losing it all. Many times that loss includes not only their savings, but their home and retirement savings as well.

While the economy, political climate, military conflicts, unemployment and even the weather can play into one's efforts to create sales, the bottom line still remains the same.

Without a good solid plan for creating sales, a business will fail.

Enter *Prospecting - Presentation - Close*. While a business may have a well written business plan, that plan must include a great deal of effort in *prospecting* for new clients, giving a persuasive *presentation* on why the prospect should buy from your company and the ability to know how to *close* the sale. Master those three and you should be successful.

In the simplest terms, you can't *close* a sale until you have made some form of a *presentation*. The catch is, you can't make that *presentation* or *close* the sale unless you are in front of a prospective buyer. Thus, constantly *prospecting* for new clients must be your top priority. If you can't get in front of a prospect, you can never make a *presentation* or more importantly, *close* a sale.

For those of you in retail sales, your *prospecting* is trying to get customers into your store. Your *presentation* is what they see when they get to your store. That would be the style of your window treatments, first impressions when they walk in the door and how they are treated as a customer. All this and more are part of a retail store's *presentation.*

Closing the sale, of course, will depend on the sales skills of your retail staff. As for closing all other types of sales, you must be a good salesperson and a closer.

By design, I have made this a short and to-the-point book. You may find it to your advantage to read this book more than once and practice some of the scenarios that have been laid out. In order to be successful in small business you are going to have to master the art of *prospecting, presentation* and *close.*

"To be successful in small business you must see yourself as a salesperson first, a business owner second."

Jerry X Shea

# Chapter 1

## Small Business Success

What line on a financial spreadsheet do you think is the most important part of running a small business? While many bankers and accountants will say it is the bottom line, the net profit (or loss) that really counts, they are wrong. Wrong because the most important line in any business spreadsheet is the very top line – Gross Sales. Gross Sales represents the total number of dollars that came into the company in any given period of time, be it daily, weekly, monthly, quarterly or yearly. While all the other lines on a spreadsheet, such as Cost of Goods, Operating Expenses, right on down to Net Profit, are, of course, important to the overall efforts of running a business, nothing else can happen in that business unless money is coming in the door. Think about that for a moment. How are you going to pay the rent, employees, fuel, utilities, insurance and all the other expenses of running a business if you don't have money coming in the door? And how does that money come in the door? That money comes into the company as a result of selling a product or service. In short, *no sales – no money.* It is that simple.

Lawyers need clients in order to provide legal assistance so they can get paid; that is their sale. Accountants need clients to pay them to do their taxes; that is their sale. Contractors need to install, fix or repair something so they can get paid; that is their sale. Every business needs to sell something in order to stay in business. You stay in business when the money coming in the door is greater than the amount of money you have to pay out for your expenses and bills. This is referred to as a positive cash flow. That money comes from the result of your sales efforts. Your inability to constantly create sales will eventually close your business down. No sales equals no income to pay your bills, employees and most important of all, no income for the owner.

To get that money coming in the door every business owner, or the person in charge of sale efforts, must understand just three words, *Prospecting - Presentation - Close.* In the simplest form *prospecting, presentation* and *close* have a backwards affect. You cannot close a sale unless you have made some form of a *presentation;* however, you cannot make that *presentation* unless you are in front of a prospective buyer. In order to get in front of that prospective buyer to make the *presentation* and to *close* the sale, you must understand the art of *prospecting.* Learn how to master all three of these and you can write your own ticket to business or sales success. Fail at any one of them and it will result in business failure. Do you, the business owner, have to be great at all three? No, but you better have great people doing the parts you don't want to do if you want to be successful in business.

# Overview

In the overall picture of business, you will have nothing without the ability to make a sale. Before you can actually make a sale, or *close* the sale (which means the sale has happened), you have to be in front of a *decision maker* to make your *presentation* or show your product.

In a retail store your *presentation* may be the way you have your merchandise displayed. For service, wholesale and manufacturing companies, your *presentation* is explaining to a prospective client your ability to perform the service, deliver the goods or manufacture the product. Before you can present your product or service, however, you need to find someone to whom you can make your *presentation*, and that takes *prospecting.* If you do not know how to *prospect*, you will never be able to make a *presentation*. If you cannot make a *presentation* that persuades the prospect to buy from you, you will never *close* the sale, or make any sales at all.

*Prospecting* for new customers should be in every business plan. No one has a business card with the title "Prospector" on it unless you're going up into the mountains each weekend looking for gold. *Prospecting* for the right client, making a great *presentation* and then *closing* the sale could indeed be like gold to everyone in your business, or in the case of a salesperson, gold for you.

The question becomes, however, who is going to do the *prospecting* for your company? If not you, who? Your inability to continually track down potential customers will suddenly bring you to the realization that you do not have enough of a customer base to stay in business. When that time comes, it will be too late. You will already be going *out-of-business*.

Every business is different, and every type of industry seeks different types of customers. *Prospecting* is really detective work. First, you have to find the names of the companies that may want your services or products. Then you have to find a way to get the name of the person in that company that has the power to make the decision to purchase your services or products. Once you have the company and the name of the decision maker (buyer), you are only half way there. Now you need to get that appointment so you can make your *presentation*. Getting that appointment, in most cases, can be a very difficult part of *prospecting* and you may find that you will be subjected to a great deal of rejection. Remember, you cannot create a sale without a *presentation*, and to make that *presentation* you need to be in front of that decision maker.

Once you get an appointment with that buyer you have to make your *presentation*. This may require overcoming any objections that the buyer may have about your product or your ability to deliver a service. Only then can you go for the *close* to try and make the sale.

Believe it or not, that last paragraph and your ability to *make the sale* may turn out to be the hardest part of owning your own business or being a salesperson. Getting in front of the decision maker and making your *presentation* is one thing. But then being told *"no thanks"* time and time again can eat away at any business owner or salesperson's self esteem.  The experienced salesperson, however, knows how to work the customer, be persuasive, overcome objections, and go for the *close* so that he or she can write the order.

One year, one of my businesses did over $50,000 dollars in business from just one client that the year before said *"no"* to me. We also did another $200,000 dollars from new customers as a result of *prospecting*. These are customers that didn't even know we existed. We didn't know that they existed either until we went looking for them. One account alone was over $45,000 dollars, and that customer had never heard of us until we called on her.

I purchased one business that someone else started and it was doing under $200,000 a year in sales. Three years later I did over $500,000. That did not happen because I was waiting for customers to come to me. It happened because I went looking for them – *prospecting*.

In order to survive in business, you will have to constantly look for new business – if for no other reason than the simple fact that you will lose business as time goes on. Clients move, companies are sold, your contact person is promoted or changed jobs. In order to survive in business you must have a written marketing plan that includes *prospecting* for new clients. If you, as a business owner do not want to do that, you need to hire a good salesperson to do it for you. What is most important is that you stick to your *prospecting* plan religiously. Failure to *prospect* for new clients equals failure in business.

"The very act of *prospecting* makes you a salesperson."

Jerry X Shea

# *Chapter 2*

## Do You Want To Be
## A Salesperson?

I was conducting a Sales & Marketing course at a business convention and explaining some selling techniques when someone at the back of the room started waving his hand in the air. I always take questions at the end of my sessions but it was obvious that this guy wanted to say something *now*. I finished my statement and addressed him by saying, *"looks like you have an important question to ask me?"* He stood up and said: *"I hate salespeople. They are always trying to push you to buy their product and I will never do that."* Keep in mind that I am conducting a seminar that teaches people how to sell and this guy has just announced to everyone that he hates salespeople.

So here is an important question for you: *"Do you hate salespeople?"* Or better yet: *"Do you want to become a salesperson?"* As I explained to the *salesperson hater* at my workshop, *"not everyone can be in sales."* If you don't want to be a salesperson, that is alright. In order to be successful in business, however, you will need to find someone that does enjoy selling and make that person your salesperson.

Let's face it, there are many types of personalities out there and not everyone is geared to become a salesperson. While many people who have never had any type of sale experience can be trained on the various sales techniques required to *close* a sale, and in time, become very good salespeople, many others, however, cannot and will not ever be good at sales (especially if they have an *"I hate salespeople"* mentality).

Here is another question for you: *"Would you like to become a telemarketer?"* If that statement makes the hair on the back of your neck stand up, guess what? You will have to become a telemarketer if you are ever going to try and sell your products to other businesses. Why? In order for you to find your prospects you are going to be making telephone calls. Those calls will be *cold calls.* That means that they did not ask you to call them. You just called them out of the blue. That's right. You will have to become one of those *telemarketers* if you want to be successful in business by creating sales. Again, if this is something you feel you can't do, just find someone who can do it. Note: there is no *"do not call list"* in the business-to-business market place.

# What *Job* Will *You* Have In Your Business?

Along with speaking at chamber of commerce workshops, business expos and small business conventions, I held workshops and was a keynote speaker to screen printers and embroiderers for the Imprint Sportswear Show (ISS) conventions across the USA for five years. I made sure that every time I stepped in front of an audience I explained to them that: *"You are not in the business of screen printing or embroidering shirts. You are in the business of making money. Screen printing or embroidery on shirts is the vehicle (at this point in your life) that makes that money. You need to think of yourself as a business owner and a salesperson, not a screen printer or embroiderer."* That goes for any business.

Unfortunately, many new business owners open a business as a result of a passion they have for something they like to do. As a result they become employees (making the product) not business people *selling* the product.

When I owned my screen printing and embroidery business back in the '90s, I was always amazed when I would run into other screen printers or embroiderers and discover that they did the screen printing or embroidery for their company. Here is the basic question. If you are doing the work, who is out selling your next job? The answer is *no one*. I owned that business for eight years and in that time over a dozen other screen printers and embroiders went *out-of-business* while we kept growing. Why? Because my job was not screen printing or embroidering; that is what my employees did. I went out and *sold* the abilities of the company. As a result we had contracts with the American Cancer Society, American Red Cross, Student Run LA, TRW, US Navy and countless large corporations and businesses, not only in my geographical area, but across the USA and even in Europe. How did we get that business? All I did day in and day out was get on the telephone and *prospect* for new clients, set appointments to make a *presentation* and then go for the *close*. In order for my employees to have a reason to come to work and earn a paycheck, they had to have something to screen print or embroider. I did not expect them to go out and sell our products, and they did not expect me to go into the back room and do the work. If I could sell, then they could print. It was that simple.

After I sold that business, my wife and I moved to Cambria, California. We had a few years of kicking back and doing nothing. We then decided to go back to work and went into real estate. We hung our real estate licenses at a company called Pines by the Sea Properties. They had nine other realtors in their office with deep roots in the community while we had none. We started on January 4, 2002. We shared a desk and each of us had a laptop. We knew very few people in town and on that first day we had no names in our date base (client list). At the end of our first year, we came in third in overall sales for the company. Other realtors that had over five years of real estate experience in Cambria could not believe how many sales we had. How did this happen? Easy, we focused on *prospecting* for clients. Was it easy? *No.* It involved a lot of work and many hours of commitment to build a real estate business. The end result, however, was well worth it. Two years later we purchased the name and goodwill of that real estate office. We also purchased the local coffee/espresso shop. We moved the real estate office into the same building as the coffee shop and found ourselves selling both coffee and real estate. How did we build our businesses? We built them by *prospecting* for new customers/clients each and every day. And we had fun doing it.

The very act of *prospecting* alone makes you a salesperson. After all, you are not tracking people down just to say "*hello.*" You are trying to locate people to whom you can sell your products or services. No matter what type of business you may be in, *prospecting* for new clients/customers must be your top priority. Once you set up a plan of action and *stick to it,* you will be amazed at the end result and the sales you will make. But you must have that action plan for *prospecting* each and every day. If you fail to constantly find new clients, you  will not create sales. No salesperson or business can survive without creating sales.

"The big pricing problem consumers have, and you have as a retailer, is: just what the heck is the actual retail price?"

Jerry X Shea

# *Chapter 3*

## How the Economy Relates to Your Small Business

Statement of fact: *Trucks, trains and airplanes cannot transport goods across the country or around the world unless sales are created.*

Stop for a moment and think of how many different manufacturers it takes to make a toaster oven. The electric cord coming out of the back of the toaster is from a vendor that makes electric cords. The two or three prong plug that goes into the electrical outlet in the wall will come from another vendor. Right there we have two vendors and all we have is a power cord ready to plug in but not attached to anything yet. Aluminum vendors will sell aluminum for the toaster oven manufacturer to make the basic toaster box. Glass companies will try to sell them glass for the front window while the manufacturers of dials, lights, switches, racks and everything else that it takes to make that toaster oven will be trying to sell their raw materials.

Once the toaster oven is made, the manufacturer sells his toasters to a distributor. The distributor finds retail outlets that want to buy the toasters. Finally, the toasters will show up in some stores. The retail store owners will then try to find buyers for their toaster ovens.

From the raw materials to the consumer buying the toaster oven there may be over a dozen sales that take place. If the retail store does not sell the toasters to the consumer, each supporting company of that toaster manufacturer suffers.

Right now, while writing this book, it is the summer of 2010 and we are in the worst economic downturn and recession since the Great Depression of the '30s. As a result, people are not spending money. That means that retail stores are not selling their merchandize. If they can't sell what they have, they are not going to buy any new inventory. Distribution companies have warehouses full of products that they can't sell to the retail store, so they are not buying from the manufacturer. The manufacturer can't create sales and cuts back on production. As a result they are not buying raw materials from their vendors. This results in companies all the way from the raw goods vendor to the retail store dismissing employees. That creates higher unemployment and some people may even lose their homes. The *domino effect* is over whelming, with many retail stores right down to manufacturing plants ending up going *out-of-business*.

Just image how many businesses have been affected because General Motors will no longer produce the Pontiac and Saturn automobiles, not to mention the closing of 2,500 GM car dealerships. The lesson learned here is simple. Price is not the issue if no one is buying.

This begs a very important question. Are you thinking of going into a business that can be affected by a negative downturn in our economy? This would not be the time to try and sell high-end items. A report published in the summer of 2009 showed that over 25 RV/motorhome manufacturers have gone *out-of-business* over the previous 18 months, not to mention all the affected RV/motorhome dealerships. These are items that in a down economy no one is rushing out to buy.

While Subway sandwiches are having a banner year selling $5 sandwiches, high-end restaurants are falling like flies. People are shopping at Wal-Mart, Costco and other big box stores, while long time department stores are folding. Between 2007 and 2009 over 25 magazines have stopped publication. A large number of local newspapers, some over 100 years old, have closed up shop because they can't get the advertizing dollars.

Whatever type of business you intend on undertaking, make sure it is a business in which the existing economy, be it up or down, will support it. If your business will be a retail store, will people buy your products at this time? If you are going to manufacture something, will the current economy justify a sale to distributors or whoever you identify as the buyer of your products? Just because you may have what you consider *a great idea for a business* does not mean that now is the time to start that business. While there are many recession proof businesses, there are also businesses that should not open in a down economy.

# How Retail Has Changed

Prior to the '70s, large department stores had two discount sales a year: the January Clearance Sale designed to sell off all the winter clothing and holiday items to get ready for the new spring line and, in July, an annual summer sale. This usually involved bedroom linens, towels and kitchen items. That was it for any discounted sales. For the other ten months out of the year items were priced at regular retail. Then things started to change. Soon there was the President's Day sale in February, Easter sale, Memorial Day sale, 4th of July sale, Labor Day sale, back to school sale, Thanksgiving sale, and now we have Black Friday (the day after Thanksgiving – who thought that one up?). Some Christmas sales start in mid-year and go all the way up to the day before Christmas and then, right after Christmas there is the ever so big day-after-Christmas sale. Suddenly, every day of the year seems to be a *sales day*.

Enter the big box stores in the '80s. While you will never see it written in words, big box stores have an unwritten goal: *put the little guy out-of-business.* While they will state that their goal is to *give the buying public quality items at a discounted price*, every time a big box store comes to town, many small businesses go *out-of-business* as they cannot compete with the very low pricing of the big box stores.

In California a company called Builders Emporium offered discounted building materials and supplies. Then Home Depot came along and did a better job at marketing its stores and put Builders Emporium *out-of-business*. While one big box store chain may have put another big box store chain *out-of-business*, between the two of them they ran just about every "mom and pop" hardware store *out-of-business*. In 1992, a Home Depot, Sam's Club and an Office Max opened in the town in which I had a small business. Within two years, five family-owned hardware stores in the surrounding area went *out-of-business*. A stationery store closed its doors after being in business for over 30 years. Countless small furniture stores, dress shops and gift stores were gone in just a couple of years. The big box stores had the ability to make large bulk purchases of their items and sell them at a lower price, a price in which the "mom and pop" stores just could not compete. The real kicker came when a large nationwide bank closed its branch right in the middle of town. Why? Because so many local small businesses had gone *out-of-business* the bank had lost the bulk of their small business accounts. Talk about a ripple effect.

By the time we entered 2000, there was no such thing as a retail price as we had known it. They became sale prices. An item that sold all over town for $10 was suddenly $5 at the big box store. That created a problem in the market place as suddenly $5 was the new retail price (at the box store) and no one could sell that item for $10 anymore in a local retail store.

Then, because all the big box stores sold the item for $5, they now had to compete with each other. So suddenly the $5 items goes on sale for $4.50 at one box store. The other box stores run advertising that states "*we will beat any other store price*" and they start selling the item for $4.35. A month goes by and one box store realizes it has a very large inventory of those items. So they include it in their Summer-Blow-Out- Sale and are now selling the item for $3.99. Will the item ever sell for $10 again? Sure, it is still selling for $10 in stores located in tourist towns and small towns miles away from the big city and box stores. As a retailer, however, you could never sell it for $10 in a town that has a box store selling it for $3.99. Since you cannot make a large bulk purchase to get your cost down so you can sell it for $3.99, you just can't afford to stock that item. If the box stores have many items that you also carry and they are selling them for 70% less than your price, you are going to be going *out-of-business.*

The big pricing problem consumers have, and you have as a retailer, is: *just what the heck is the real retail price?* If an item is marked $10 as the retail price, but has a discount sticker on that says $3.99, what is the price? Obviously, the price is $3.99. But wait, what does the $10 represent? The answer may surprise you. The box store knows that the out of town stores sell the item for $10. So the box stores make $10 their *marked retail price.* Then with the store's big 70% discount, they mark it down to $3.99. The truth is, they never had a price of $10. They are just using that to make the consumers think they are getting a big discount. Can you, the small retailer do that? Yes, you can. You do what the big chain stores do and mark up your inventory to an ultra high retail price. Then put a *discount sticker* on it at a lower price. In short, you take that $10 item, mark it up to $15, and put a discount sticker on it for $8.99. It doesn't matter if the consumer knows it sell for $10 at another store, you are selling it for $8.99 and to them, that is a good deal. Keep in mind that if a consumer has to drive 150 miles to a big box store, the $8.99 price is then a discounted price for their town.

Now you may not be able to take a gift item and mark it up ten times to get your *artificial retail price.* But you can sure mark it up five times and put a discount sticker on it for a lower sales price. If, however, your small gift store is sur-rounded by a number of discount box stores all selling the same item for a much lower price, the end may be near for your store.

Your only hope of staying in business is to find items that the big box stores do not carry. Consumers are looking for those items and you can price them to sell and still make a profit.

Understanding how to price your retail items and how to market your store when you are in competition with larger stores is paramount to your ability to stay in business.

"A lack of sales can easily be traced to a business owner's failure to effectively market his product or service."

Jerry X Shea

# Chapter 4

## Sales and Marketing Tools

## Business Cards

Without a doubt, the single most misunderstood and least expensive form of marketing any company is the business card. Here is an item that contains your name, the name of your company, your address, telephone number, fax number, and e-mail address. Yet, with all of this important information on one card, how many times have you asked a person for his business card only to be told: *"Oh,- I don't have one on me."* My answer to that statement is: *"How can you call yourself a business person when you don't even carry a business card?"* Why would any business owner who wants to succeed in business not want to make sure that she is carrying a business card with her at all times? The answer is simple. She does not perceive a business card as a marketing tool and doesn't have a plan for its use. This is really unfortunate since the business card can be the most powerful means of advertising your business.

The smart business owner carries business cards in her purse, car, briefcase, home and office. You would not believe the number of times I have met with someone at his or her place of business, asked for a business card only to be told: *"Oh, I can't seem to find one."*

Distributing your business cards to every person who will take it and at every location that will accept it is crucial to your succeeding in business. When you go out to eat, tip the waiter and hand him your card telling him that if he ever needs your product or service, to give you a call. Leave a card on every bulletin board in a public bathroom, grocery store, and drug store every time you walk in. Leave a card at all of the places that you attend. If you go to your kid's little league game, walk the stands, introduce yourself, tell them your kid's name and number (on their jersey), and hand every parent a business card. Tell them what you do. NOTE: Do not become a business card *litterer*. Don't throw your cards into a crowd of people at a sports game or place them in an inappropriate place. You could be fined for littering. After all, your name and phone number are on the card.

Here is one word of caution to new business owners. If you take a good look at all of the business cards you can find, you will notice that most are just black print on a white card - very simple. Unless the card is from a graphics company or has a photo of the person such as a insurance or real estate card, you will not find a lot of full-color cards. You do not need to spend the money for a full-color or multi-color card for your business. If you want color on your card or letter-head (other than black) do not put more than one other color on your card. Remember, you can get 1,000 business cards printed for less then $20. You could spend over $500 for the set up alone of a full color business card and letterhead. Beware of a friend that likes to work with computer art and offers to design a card for you. Your friend may design a great card. It may, however, be so expensive to print that it will put you in the poor house. Also, it is cost prohibitive to print 1,000 business cards on your computer when a printing company can do the job for less.

It may be just another business card to a lot of people, but in the hands of the right people, it represents the future of your company. Your job is to get those cards into those hands as quickly as you can. You do that by setting a goal to make sure you hand out at least 6 cards a day. It should not be hard. If you do that, you will have handed out 1,000 cards by the end of your first sixth month in business. The odds are in your favor that someone who received your card will call you or go to your business. Don't underestimate the power of that little card.

If you are doing your job correctly and passing out your business cards all of the time, you will be ready to order more cards in about 6 months. If it is the end of your first year in business and you still have a full box of business cards, I will bet that you are about to go *out-of-business*. If you don't believe me, just look for a company that has just gone *out-of-business* and see what they throw in the trash – boxes of business cards.

Do not print one-sided business cards. Make sure you have a two-sided card. While the front will have all of the basic information, the back of your card is an excellent place to put a statement, photo, quote or anything else you want that will make your card stand out from the rest. When you hand someone your card, always hand it to them with the back side up (so they see that first). With a unique statement or image on that card, believe me when I say: *"They will remember your card."*

# Fliers

Every business needs to have a marketing program that includes sending out an advertising flier. Yes, I know, there's another hand going up and someone saying: *"I hate junk mail."* Sure, everyone says that they hate junk mail. But admit it, you have received junk mail and there have been times when you kept that flier from some business, saying to yourself: *"I might need that some day."* Go ahead, admit it.

Like a business card, a business flier is another way to *put your business out there.* But here is the key to a good marketing campaign with a flier. Do not do a blind mailing. Mailing out a flier to zip codes in areas that you have not driven around in to see the homes or businesses that are there is a waste of your money. Why would someone that has a carpet cleaning business want to send fliers to a neighborhood with cars up on blocks in the front yard, houses that need painting and roofs with shingles missing? You want your fliers to go to affluent neighborhoods if you are selling home services.

Along with having a flier to mail out, use them to hand out to people. Giving someone a business card and a flier at the same time will help that person remember you.

# Catalogs

A small business cannot afford to put together a 50-page color catalog. That does not mean you can't have one. Many times, the vendors and suppliers to your industry publish catalogs you can buy, put your company sticker on them and *voila*, you have a catalog. Some companies will even print your name on the front and back cover (for a fee) and you have what really looks like your company catalog. This is something you really do need to check out. When dealing with a prospective buyer, you will really raise the buyer's perception of your company with a catalog. For six years I used a vendor's catalog imprinted with my company logo and address. Those catalogs created such a positive image of my company that when I went out to make a *presentation*, I blew my competition right out of the water.

# Internet

Just because there is an internet does not mean that you have to sell on it. It would be a great goal if in a few years you have a real up and running internet business. For now, however, just get an internet presence with your phone number and address. Getting ripped off from bad credit cards, returned items, shipping problem are all a part of an internet business. If you are just starting a home town business, stay focused on finding local business before you try reaching the whole world. If you spend more than $500 for a website and domain name, you over spent.

Depending on your business, you may want to set up a blog or even a presence on a business networking site. But doing so will only be for the benefit of *getting your company name out there*. Don't think that having an internet presence will make you a millionaire.

# Chamber of Commerce – Networking

I ran into a business owner once who said he use to belong to his local chamber of commerce but *"they never gave me any business."* Folks, the purpose of a chamber of commerce is not to give anyone business; it is to give every business an opportunity to network with other businesses. I cannot encourage you enough to join your local chamber of commerce and *work it* to help establish your business in the community. Every chamber of commerce usually has a monthly mixer. Go to it with a box full of business cards and fliers. Walk up to everyone in that room, introduce yourself and hand them a card and flier. Get to know as many other business owners as you can. Get their business cards (don't be surprised when they say, *"oh, I don't have one on me"*) and start a file for all the businesses in your area. You may not sell anything to one particular business, but someone might ask that business owner for the name of a company that sells what you sell, and that owner could recommend you. But that will only happen if you have done your part to make sure that business owners know you and your business exist. If you work the chamber of commerce to your advantage you will be surprised at the referrals you may get.

# Other Businesses Just Like Yours

You are not at war with other businesses just like yours. You are all in competition with each other. That does not mean that you cannot go and talk with other owners. If you are just starting out in business, go around to the other well-established businesses, introduce yourself and tell them that if they ever get a request for a job/product/service that is too small for them, you would appreciate the referral. You may be very surprised when the phone rings and someone says that another company recommended your company. Many times, as businesses grow, it is not cost effective to work on a small job when they have the capacity to do large jobs. You, however, cannot do a large job, but can do the small ones. Of course, if someone wants you to do a job that is out of your realm, you would return the favor by recommending the larger company.

# Get Your Company Name Out There

Are you ashamed of what you do for a living? I hope not. Real estate people are not ashamed of what they do so they put their company name and their name on their car. Is anyone in construction ashamed of what they do? They have their company name plastered all over their trucks, vans and cars. So if you are not ashamed of what you do, why not put your company name on your car? It can be anything from a simple magnetic billboard that you can put on your car door or the full on signage all over the car/van and windows. If you are truly serious about your business/profession, you need to billboard your car.

There are many marketing tools that you can use to help keep your company name in the public eye, such as pens, calendars, coffee mugs, t-shirts and more. Don't get carried away, but a simple little something with your company name on it that can be handed out to a prospect could be useful to the person and just helps to *gets your name out there.*

# Produce a Company Newsletter

When I owned my screen printing/embroidery company, my real estate business and then the coffee/espresso shop,

I put out a newsletter every six months. It was printed on a 17 x 11 glossy stock paper and when folded in half it became an 8 ½ x 11, four-sided newsletter. It was then folded down again to 8 ½ x 5 ½ for mailing. The front page contained three stories related to the particular business. The left inside page contained statistics for the industry, and the inside right page had additional space for the front stories and some photos. On the back side, I had a puzzle at the top, the return address and mailing label spot (when folded down). People could submit the answer to the puzzle by email for a chance to win dinner for two at a local restaurant. The puzzle was a big hit.

The concept of a newsletter is simple. Once you set up the format, it is really easy to knock out another newsletter six months later. Just keep collecting articles, stories and anything you think would be of interest to your clients. Be sure to give credit to the appropriate person for anything written by someone else.

Along with mailing it to all your clients, do you remember those business cards you collected at the chamber of commerce mixer? Hopefully you have entered all those names and businesses into your computer data base and can also print out mailing labels to them.

The newsletter is another tool to help keep your company name in the eye of all your clients that you already have and any new prospects out there. It is a great reminder to them of who you are and what your company does.

# Volunteer

A really great way to get your name out there is to volunteer to do something at an event. Take a stack of business cards with you and volunteer to be a bartender at a fund raising event. Because you are volunteering you will be surprised at how many people will ask you, *"so what do you do?"* With your business cards right there on the bar, tell them to take one and tell them what you do. How simple is that? Is there a local charity golf game coming up? If so, volunteer to help out. What about a 10k run? Running events always need help and volunteers. Look for a church or school activity that could use volunteers. Your kid's little league games always need people to help set-up. Just find some event that you can give a little of your time as a volunteer and take advantage of the opportunity to meet and greet what could turn out to be prospective clients.

Volunteer to do highway clean-up. Here is an excellent photo opportunity. Volunteer to help clean-up the highway in your town. Make sure you take a camera and have someone take a group photo. Submit that photo to the local newspaper. They are always looking for community involvement photos and stories. Make sure you include your name and what company you are from. Also put it in your newsletter. I performed highway clean up every month for five years as a realtor. It was another great way to keep my name and company in the public eye. Of course, I was always very pleased when someone would come up to me at the market and say: *"I saw your picture in the newspaper. Thanks for keeping our highway clean."*

# Monitor What You Do

Whatever it is that you do or *put out there,* you must monitor the results to assess if it is working. By having a puzzle contest on the back of my newsletters I could tell by the number of responses by folks trying to win a dinner if, in fact, my newsletter was *getting out there.*

When someone calls you, always ask, *"how did you get our number?"* If you are in a couple of yellow page directories, ask on what page they found you. If you get a lot of calls from page 627 in one yellow page directory, but hardly ever get a call from page 837 in another yellow page directory, drop the yellow page advertising with the fewer results.

# Call Ed

Each time I made up a flier I had a code on it. My code was a fictitious telephone extension or the name of a person. When I would get a call off of the flier and someone would ask to speak to "Ed," I would just say *"Ed is not here right now, but I can help you."* Because they asked for Ed, I knew what flier they were calling from. If they asked for "extension 220" (of which there was none), I knew what flier generated that call. If they did not ask for a name or extension, I would ask: *"What name [or extension] are you looking for?"* That way I could tell what fliers worked and which ones did not work. If I did not get any calls for Ed, I would not send fliers to that industry or zip code area again.

To spend money in advertising and not know if it is working is a waste of your money. Monitor everything you do. If it brings in business, keep doing it. If you cannot justify the amount of business you get from any form of advertising, drop it.

# Sales and Marketing Punch List

____    Business Card (hand out 6 a day)
____    Fliers (to go with your business card
____    Catalog
____    Internet
____    Join the Chamber of Commerce
____    Check out other businesses like yours
____    Get your company name out there
____    Produce a company newsletter
____    Monitor all your advertising (ask for Ed)
____    Volunteer in your community


____    _____


____    _____

"The ongoing success of your business is directly proportional to your ability to constantly find new prospects."

Jerry X Shea

# *Chapter 5*

## Finding the Prospect

You have opened your business. You have your business cards (printed on both sides), a flier, a catalog, you joined the chamber of commerce and you are ready for business. Now what? What is it going to take to get that phone to ring? When will customers start coming through the door? When will the cash register go *ka-ching*? The answer to that is *"when you start prospecting."* How do you start *prospecting?* On your first day in business you pick up the phone and start calling prospective business clients who you think might need or use your product/service.

How do you find these prospective clients? You read the local paper every day. If you have a business that provides a service, you look for any business listed or described in the paper that you feel will need the service you provide. If you produce or sell a product, you look in the paper for a company or person that could use the product that you sell. Many times the article will give the name of the very person in that company that you need to call. You may even be able to refine your search quicker by using the internet.

If you are in manufacturing, go to your local library and get your hands on business directories that list businesses, owner names or the person in that company that may be the buyer for what you produce or sell. The key here is that you arc looking (*prospecting*) for anyone in that company that can use what you have to sell. Thus, you are looking for a contact person so you can set an appointment to make your *presentation.*

# Walk the Industrial Parks

With business cards, fliers and catalogs in hand you need to walk into every business park that you can find. I made that my Tuesday and Thursday job when I owned my screen printing and embroidery company. Some days I would not show up at the office until 3 p.m. because I was walking the industrial parks.

You have something to sell and you have to take the position that every business out there needs, and wants, what you have to offer. If they don't need what you have to sell, they will tell you. But don't ever assume that they don't need it. Assume they do need it until they tell you otherwise.

Walk into each office and just introduce yourself. Ask to speak to the person who buys what you sell. Some people may be the owner of that business and will most likely listen to what you have to say. A receptionist may ask you to leave your card and, if interested, someone will contact you later.

This is the time to ask: *"and what is the name of the person who will be calling me?"* You want that name so you know who to contact later. Don't leave without it.

When you see a sign that reads *"No Soliciting"* please keep in mind that *"No Soliciting"* is French for *"Come on in."* OK, so that is not what it means. If you want to know the real definition, look it up in the dictionary. You might be surprised. What it means to you, however, is that there is a business on the other side of that door and you need to find out if that business could use what you have to sell. The only way that will happen is if you walk through that door. I have never heard of anyone being shot to death because he entered a business that had a *"No Soliciting"* sign out front. Just walk in and ask the receptionist or whomever you run into for the name of the person who buys your product or services for the company. Get the name and ask if you can see him or her. If the person says *"no,"* that is OK. Thank them and leave. Now you have the name of someone at that company to call, send a flier and make an appointment to go back and see.

If you make it a goal to walk every industrial park you can find, introduce yourself or get the name of a contact person, and then follow up with a phone call, your business will grow.

# Scenario #1

You feel that the ABC company across town could use what your business sells. You even have the name of the contact person. So you make the call. You get a receptionist. You ask for Mr./Ms. _____ and she says: *"He [she] is not in the office right now. Would you like his [her] voice mail?"* Your answer: *"Yes, please."* Now, what are you going to say in your message? This is a make it or break it situation. You may only get one shot at impressing your prospect enough that he or she will take your call when you call again. NOTE: Do not leave the following message: *"Call me at 555-5555."* Their work day does not include returning cold calls. But, your goal is to leave the kind of message that will impress them enough that they *will* take your call when you call back later.

Because there are so many different types of businesses and business needs, I cannot tell you what to say about your business or service. But I can say, however, it is very important that when you leave your message, it must sound sincere (not sound like you are reading a script). You must also speak in a tone that makes the prospect want to hear more.

Here are a few samples;

- *"My name is _____ from _____ and I understand that you are the buyer for [what you want to sell them]. I will be stopping by your business on Thursday afternoon and I look forward to meeting you and showing you our company products."*
- *"Hello _____, my name is _____. Our company, _____, has a product that I'm sure you will find of interest for your company. I will call back tomorrow to set up an appointment to stop by to see you and show you this product."*

- *"Hi _____ . Sorry I missed you, but I hope to see you next time I stop by so I can show you our company's product line. My name is _____ and I am from _____."*
- *"Hi _____ . I have some **great news** for you. My name is _____ and I will call you back tomorrow to tell you about it."* (Your great news is that you have something his company needs.)

Once you make that call and leave a message it is very important that you indeed follow up. Go to the business on Thursday. Make that follow-up call. Keep in mind that you may call over ten times and still never get to talk to the prospect. Then one day, he/she picks up the phone. Now what will you say?

Again, I cannot tell you what to say, but I can tell you that if you don't say the right things, you lost your prospect. Remember, you can't sell anything over the telephone unless you are doing direct telephone sales. You are making the call because you are trying to get a face-to-face meeting to give your presentation and show what your company has to offer them. It is the first step in creating that sale.

Will you get every appointment? *No.* It is a game of odds. The more calls you make to different prospects, the better the chances are that you will get an appointment with one of them. If you find you are not getting any appointments, you are saying the wrong things in your telephone calls. You may need some telephone sales training. There are many sales training seminars that are put on all across the country. You may have to undergo some intense training in telephone sales to get those appointments.

# Understanding the Gate Keeper

You will find that as you are *prospecting* for new clients, the bigger the company, the harder it will be to get to that buyer or decision maker. In some large organizations a receptionist or secretary to the person you are trying to get to see will act as the *gate keeper*. Part of his or her job is to protect the boss from unwanted calls and/or from people that are trying to get an unsolicited meeting with the boss. Thus, *the gate keeper holds the keys to the gate.* Get past the gate keeper and you will have a meeting with the person he or she is protecting. So how do you get past the gate keeper? It is not easy, but it can be done.

First, who is the gate keeper? What is his/her name? Once you have the name, you can start addressing the person by his or her name. That is a plus for you. How do you find the name? Ask someone else in the company. If you think the person you are trying to reach has a secretary, call the front desk and ask the receptionist for the name of that person's secretary. Now when you call, ask for her. When she answers, address her by name and confirm (with her) that she is indeed Mr./Ms.____ secretary. What you need to do is to sell her on why she should set an appointment for you to see her boss. That, in and of itself, may be the hardest thing you will ever do.

Gate keepers can be the receptionist out front, a partner or another business owner within the company, the secretary, an office manager, a co-worker or anyone that is *in charge of keeping sales people away*. This does not mean that the company never meets with any salespeople. It just means that, if you really do have a product or service that you feel the company could use, you have your work cut out for you as you try to get that meeting set up. Do everything you can to get to that decision maker. Remember, someone from some company *will* get to that prospect. Any reason why it should not be you?

# Who Are You?

Speaking of *you*, it is really important to keep in mind that the best *prospecting* tool your company has is *you.* It is your business and no one knows it better than you. But wait. You know *you*, but how many other people know *you*? Let's imagine that I came to your town and decided to open a new business. While in town, I go to the local barber shop, the very one, in fact, that you go to for your hair cut. While getting my hair cut I ask the barber: *"Say, I need to find a company that sells _____ [what you, the reader, are selling]. Who can you recommend?"* Will that barber give me your company name along with your business card or the card of your competitor? If it is not your card, you are not doing a good job of selling *you* and your company. The same goes if I ask the guy behind the counter at the local deli, the dry cleaner, coffee shop or your favorite restaurant. If the places you patronize don't know what you do, you are not doing your job when it comes to marketing *you* and your company.

To find out how you are doing on that, the next time you go to you barber/salon, ask the barber/beautician: *"Do you know what I do for a living?"* If he/she says *"yes"* and has your business cards in their drawer, good for you. If, however, he/she says: *"No, what do you do?"* Shame on you for going to the same places on a regular basis and the people there don't even know what you do. Tell the barber/beautician what you do. Hand him/her a stack of your business cards and ask him/her to please pass your card on to any person looking for your product or service. In return, ask him/her for a stack of his/her business cards, promising to pass them on to anyone looking for a barber/beauty shop. This is a win-win for both of you and you should be doing it with all the places you frequent. Get your business cards out there. It is another great way to prospect for new clients. And, by getting their business cards, you are building your data base of contacts for your newsletters and fliers.

Most importantly, start selling *you*. Just think of the people, right now, that you don't even know very well yet you know what they do for a living. Your goal is to become someone who everyone in your community remembers and knows what you do for a living, even if they don't know you personally.

# You and Your Mouth

Just like billboarding your car, your mouth can say a lot about your business. In short, talk about your business and what you do as often as you can. The longer you are in business, the more *business stories* you will have to tell people about. A great story to tell others is one about a customer who was really happy with your product or service. Maybe there was a time when something broke or fell apart and you *saved the day* with a quick fix. Every business has stories and you should tell yours whenever you can. When you attend a wedding, you have a captive audience right there at that table for 10. You never know who is sitting right in front of you who could use your product or service. So talk it up. Social functions, neighborhood parties, and any get-togethers are great vehicles to do just that. They open the door for you to talk about your business. So talk it up.

NOTE: It is very important that your spouse understand what you are doing when you talk about your business at a social event. If he or she says: *"Oh please don't talk about your company,"* then you need to have a little *sit down* and explain why you do it. Also keep in mind that at a social event it is not the time to brag or boast about something in your business. Saying, *"I just closed the biggest deal and made a lot of money"* would be a very inappropriate statement.

# Find Your Niche and Work It To Death

What many small business owners fail to realize is that they have hundreds of prospects right under their nose. Who are those prospects? They are the other *businesses* of the same type that they are selling to right now. For the sake of this example, let's say you are selling a product or service to a construction company. If you have one construction company customer, how many other construction companies do you think are doing the same thing and could also use your product/service? If you really start to dig deep into that industry you may find hundreds, even thousands, of other companies that could also use what you have to sell. This is called _finding your nitch and working it to death._ Find the names and numbers of everyone in that industry and contact each and every one of them. Yes, each and everyone. This is your market and you need to work it constantly. You can have as many markets (niches) as you can handle, but just keep going after all the prospects in each niche.

When I owned my screen printing/embroidery company, I identified the weekend running events (5k, 10k, and marathon) as one of my niches. A few years later our company was screen printing over 80% of the running events in the Los Angeles and Orange County area. This did not happen because these event people came to us. It was because we went to them to get the business.

# Never Pre-Qualify Your Prospect

Want to go out of business real quick? Just decide to wait on customers based on how they look or dress. To judge others by their outward appearance is the _kiss of death_ for any salesperson. In most sales situations, everyone you meet is a prospective buyer. Just because someone is dressed in old pants and shoes does not mean that he or she is not capable of buying your product. If you think all millionaires dress in fancy clothing, guess again. I have made sales to people that were very well off financially, but dress, by choice, as if they were homeless. If you ask the correct questions up front, you can usually ascertain if that prospect has the buying power to purchase what you are selling. But, to look at someone and say to yourself, *"Oh, they can't afford it"* may only result in a lost opportunity to make a sale. Never pre-qualify.

"If you have a *fear of public speaking* you need to learn how to overcome it. Otherwise, you will crash and burn big time when you are presenting your product to a group."

Jerry X Shea

# *Chapter 6*

## The Presentation - Can You Do It?

Your *prospecting* has paid off and you have set an appointment to go and meet with a prospective buyer. You will be making your *presentation* tomorrow at 2 p.m. Here is the million dollar question: Do you have a great *presentation* about your company and the product(s) you sell? If not, you will not get the business. You have to understand that you are not the only person out there trying to sell something to this company. You have to give that prospect a good reason to buy from you and not from some other company.

# The Greeting and Handshake

Your presentation will start the second you walk into the room and your eyes meet those of your prospect. Remember, you are selling *you* and your company's capabilities to deliver a product or service. Selling *you* starts with that handshake. Do you know how to shake hands correctly? That might seem like a stupid question, but you would be amazed at the people I meet who do not know how to shake hands correctly.

A poor handshake is a set-up for a failed presentation. Shaking hands and looking down at your prospect's feet are sure signs that you lack confidence. Some people think that a strong handshake means squeezing the prospect's hand. Wrong again. Bringing your prospect to his or her knees is not a nice way to meet and greet anyone, especially a woman. Standing there pumping the prospect's hand up and down as if you were trying to get water to come out of their mouth is also a sign of insecurity. The "dead fish" hand shake, no motion or life to the hand, is just another sign of insecurity. You must remember that this prospect may meet with a dozen people each day who are also trying to sell something to his or her company. That person knows what a confident hand shake feels like. Here is a special note for men about shaking the hand of a woman. That big hand of yours that can crush a beer can also crush the knuckles of most women. Never shake the hand of a woman with the same strength that you would shake the hand of a man. OK, sure you may meet a woman twice your size. When that happens, just match the strength of her hand shake. But if you want to kill your chance of a comfortable *meet and great*, just bust the knuckles of a woman prospect. As for you women shaking hands with a man, hand him a "dead fish" hand shake and you will not be making any points. Learn how to present your hand with a firm (not knuckle breaking) grasp and commanding shake, and you will score big points.

Along with the handshake comes your body language. It is imperative that you look the prospect straight in the eye (the right eye – same side as the handshake), shake the hand up and down only two times and then let loose. People know the feel of a good handshake that comes from a confident person, compared to a poor, wet-weak handshake from a nervous vendor. If you are not sure of what your handshake is like, shake hands with friends and relatives and ask them to help you develop the right handshake. A good handshake sets the tone of your meeting. You only have a few seconds to make that positive impression, that is, from your first eye contact as you enter the room to the end of your handshake. Shake hands correctly and you made your first points in your *presentation.*

Special Note: If you are the type that has a wet hand (usually from being nervous) do not put baby powder on your hands just before you meet someone. You will smell like a diaper when you walk into the room, not to mention leaving baby powder on your prospect's hand. Stay away from scented hand wipes. You'll smell like your day job is at the car wash. If you need to dry your hands, wipe your hand with a handkerchief just before you walk into the room and wave your hand in the air a few times. Then walk in and shake hands.

# To Whom Are
# You Presenting?

Depending on what it is that your company is selling, you may find that there are times when your *presentation* is not to just one person, but to a committee or even a board of directors. Again, you will be trying to sell yourself and your company's products or services.

# Scenario #2

You have set an appointment with a company to make your *presentation* tomorrow at 10 a.m. This time, however, instead of presenting to just one person you will be presenting to a committee of four. On top of that, you will be the first of three people presenting that morning. You will be given 10 minutes for your *presentation*. As soon as you hear that you will be presenting to more than one person and that you are one of three making a presentation that day, your *presentation* skills must jump ten-fold. Now, instead of dealing with one personality, you have to deal with four personalities. And, you are in competition with two other companies. Can this really happen? You bet it can, and it does quite often.

You get there on time and are taken into a room in which four people are seated around the end of a table. You are at the head of the table with about 6-8 feet between you and the others. It could be awkward to try and shake hands with everyone. This is a situation in which you have to analyze the set up and realize quickly that handshaking may be out of the question. All eyes are on you and you start with *"Good morning everyone, I am _____ from _____."* With that you start your *presentation.*

NOTE: As with any *presentation,* you should know what product they are interested in, how many they want and when they want it delivered. Make sure you confirm that with the group. It will show that you did the correct research and assures them that everyone is on the *same page.*

Here is the problem you will have when you give a group *presentation.* First, can you win over everyone in the room? Say one thing that rubs someone the wrong way and that person will not vote for your company. Because you are the first to present, you must make such a positive impression on each one of them that they will use your *presentation* to judge the other two presenters. NOTE: If you should be the second or third presenter, you still need to make sure that your *presentation* is the one they remember and like the best.

But here is the real problem. Will you know how to respond to the four different personalities in that room? Let us go around the table and take a look at each one of these people.

- The guy sitting to your left is sitting back in his chair with his arms folded and resting on his chest.
- Next to him is a lady holding a large yellow lined note pad with pen in hand. She will be writing down every word you say.
- At the far end of the table is a guy sitting upright in his chair, elbows on the table and his hands together.

- On the right side of the table is a lady without any expression on her face. Her hands are folded on her lap.

Now, who do you think is in charge of this meeting? Better yet, who will make the final decision and can override the others?

If you think the above is made up, guess again. I have been through *presentations* with as many as twelve people in the room and each one with a different personality. Talk about a hard sell. That type of *presentation* is the ultimate *you* having to *"sell yourself."* Everyone presenting that day has basically the same products. Yes, price will play into the equation and we will address that later. For now, you have to focus on selling *you*.

Here are a few examples of selling yourself, which really means you win them over so they feel comfortable buying from you.

- While making your *presentation*, you say "my wife/ husband asked me yesterday _____ [you fill in the blank] or my daughter asked me _____[you fill in the blank]." What you are doing here is establishing, in a subtle way, that you are a married family man/ woman that is trying to raise and support a family. As much as you might think *"oh, who cares,"* think again. Remember you are selling yourself.
- If you are single, try to work in your relationship with your parents. Don't reference a boy or girl friend. Remember, you are selling *you*. Let them know that you love your *family*. A short 10-second statement about anything involving your family will just help establish your image of that nice boy/ girl next door trying to make it on his or her own.

- If you are young (married or single) and are talking to a group of much older people, try to talk about your grandmother/grandfather. Something like, "my grandfather always said: "_____." (It is your grandfather, so what great advice did he give you?) Show them how you respect older people.
- If you are in a Rotary, Lions, Toastmasters or any club, mention it. Who knows, one of those decision makers may also be in the same type of club and would like to give the business to one of their own.

Whatever you say, DO NOT give a *poor me* story. No one will buy from you if you tell them you are about to lose your home, or your son is on drugs, your spouse is leaving you, your parents won't talk to you, you had a car accident on the way over or any other sob story. That is a guaranteed *sales killer.*

So let's get back to our committee of four. Who do you think is the person in charge? Mr. arms folded? Ms. pen in hand? The person at the top end of the table with his elbows on the table? Or Ms. no expression?

Here is the catch. None of them. That's right, *none* of them have the final say as to which company will be hired. These four people are called *"recommenders,"* a committee of four that are interviewing prospective vendors and will make its *recommendation* to the final decision maker or even worse, a larger committee.

You may have walked out of that *presentation* high-fiving yourself because it was one of the best *presentations* you ever gave. You did and said everything so right that even you can't believe it went so well. But there is one really big problem and it is indeed *your problem*. Do you think the *committee* can repeat your great *presentation* to the final decision maker(s)? The answer is simple. *No,* it cannot. It was your *presentation* and the committee is not going to give your *presentation* to someone else.

So let me ask you again. As much as your *presentation* has to be right on the money, will the committee recommend your *presentation* or will it recommend *you?* The answer, of course, is *you.* If your product satisfies their need, they will recommend *you* and your company, based upon *you* and your *presentation.*

Let us assume that the other two presenters gave basically the same type of *presentation.* All of you have the same product. Your pricing is about the same. So who should they hire? Believe me when I say they will hire the company that not only put on the best *presentation,* but the company that had the person they all felt that they could relate to in whatever way that may have been. They will remember the person and the company that, when they meet with the decision maker(s) to give their report, won them over and they remember the best. It will be the person and the company with which they feel most *comfortable.* That sense of comfort will come from *you. You* represent the company that will give them what they need. *That is a statement of fact, and you can take it to the bank.*

In time, you are going to find that there are many different conditions that may affect a *presentation.* The bottom line, however, is really easy. Your *presentation* must be top notch. *You,* as the presenter, have to be very sharp at overcoming any objections that might come up. You must be able to give clean and precise answers to any questions about your company and the product(s) you are selling. If someone asks you a question and you are unable to answer it quickly, that person will know that you don't know the answer. If you say, *"I'll have to get back to you on that,"* you're dead. This is especially true if they ask the same question to any of the other presenters and they answer the question immediately. Remember Ms. yellow pad and pen? When she gives her part of the report, she will have noted that you did not know the answer to a question while the other presenters were able to answer it. One slip up, and believe me when I say *you will know when it happens,* and you will lose the sale.

# Use Your Listening Skills To Become a Problem Solver

There will be many times in which you will meet with a prospect to find out what it is that your prospect wants to buy in the future. This means you have to listen to what the prospect says and then form your response based on what he said. You will not be going from a *presentation* into a *close* as you don't really know yet just what it is you will be selling. To get to that sale will require excellent listening skills. You must learn to listen closely to your prospect to understand just exactly what it is the prospect is looking for or needs to buy. If your prospect tells you what he or she wants and you give him or her pricing based on something else or on something they told you they do not want, you will lose the chance for a sale.

When you take the position of a *problem solver*, you will be amazed at the number of times your prospect buys from you. The key here is that your prospect has a *problem*. The problem is that the prospect needs to buy something that you sell so that he/she can continue on with his/her business. When you meet and give your *presentation* on your product line or service, you will also hear from them as to what it is they are really looking for and need. As a *problem solver*, you are going to help them solve that problem. So tell them that you are a problem solver.

*"Mr./Ms. if I understand you correctly, your problem is that you don't have [your product or service] and you are looking for a company that can help you solve that problem by providing that [product/service]. Is that correct?"* That statement will get you a great response. It shows your prospect that you have been listening to just what the problem is and you are there to help him or her solve it.

Many times you will just gather information at the first meeting that you then take back to your company to put together the final *presentation.* But you better make sure you know exactly what it is the prospect really wants. Come back with a *presentation* that does not hit the nail on the head and you will lose the sale.

Great listening skills are paramount to your success. Never open your mouth when the prospect is speaking – *NEVER.* If you cut them off by jumping in with a statement while the prospect is talking, you are NOT listening to them. Listen, make notes and respond when the prospect is finished.

# Only Ask
# Open-Ended Questions

As you investigate the needs of your prospect, make sure that you ask only open-ended questions. The difference between an open-ended question and a closed-end question is how the prospect answers the question. Here are two examples.

Closed-end: *"Sir, do you like this red color?"* The problem is that question elicits a *"yes"* or *"no"* answer, which will not tell you what he thinks of that color other than he either likes it or doesn't like it. Open-ended: *"Sir, what do you **think** of this color?"* He cannot answer *"yes"* or "*no.*" He has to respond to the question with a longer answer. That answer will help you define just what the prospect likes or doesn't like (in this case, about the color red).

Never say: *"Do you like this?" "Is this what you are looking for?" "Is this OK?" "How about this?"* Never ask a question that will get a *"yes"* or *"no"* answer. The correct questions are: "*What do you think of this?" "How would this work?" "Here are a few colors. Which one stand out best for you?"* The idea is to ask an open-ended question in which the prospect must reveal more of what he or she is thinking or feeling. A *"yes"* or *"no"* response to a closed-end question gives you very little information to work with in trying to meet the prospect's need.

# The Overkill Presentation

I had a friend who was trying to develop a product line. He had some great ideas and had an opportunity to present his line to a buyer of a very large store. When all was said and done, he did not get to write an order. I asked him to stop by and give his *presentation* to me after work one day. I sat there making some notes while he gave his *presentation.* I never said a word, did not interrupt him or asked any questions. Forty-five minutes later, he finished his *presentation.* Let me make it real clear to you, the readers, as I did to him that day. **He was dead when he hit the ten minute mark and said, *"now I would like to show you --------."*** All I could think of was: What do you mean, *"now I would like to show you ----."* You have been talking for ten minutes and there is *more?* And there was more, twenty minutes, thirty minutes, forty minutes later and there was still more. There was no doubt in my mind that his product had potential, but his *presentation* was killing the deal.

No one, and I do mean *no one,* who buys products is going to sit through a *presentation* that seems as if it will never end, let alone one that is over ten minutes (unless the prospect has scheduled you for a longer period of time).

Whatever you are trying to sell, if you cannot present it in five to ten minutes, you will never write a job order. These buyers meet with people all day long and they are not going to sit and listen to a *presentation* that is over ten minutes, let alone close to an hour. The ideal *presentation* should be five to ten minutes and should have only four parts:

1.  Who are you (and the name of your business)?
2.  What are the products/services you are trying to sell?
3.  Why they should buy from you and your company?
4.  What is your price?

That is it. Short, sweet and to the point. That *presentation*, however, must exceed their expectations. Stand out from the others. You need to give them a real good reason to buy from you and your company and not from someone else. Give that type of a *presentation* and you are half way to a written deal.

Back in the '80s, I worked for a company that set up appointments for other businesses. It was a great concept. We set up the appointments and then sold the appointments to companies that wanted more business. This was a great service for small companies that did not want to go out *prospecting* for new business. But there was a big problem. We could find the company that, as an example, needed janitorial services. Thus, we had a prospect. We would tell that company that we would send three janitorial companies over for them to interview. We set the appointments. We would then find janitorial companies in the prospect's area that wanted some work and agreed to go over and give their *presentation* to the prospect. Obviously, the salesperson who could sell its company's abilities to do the janitorial work to the satisfaction of the prospect would get the order.

I remember one case in which we received a call from a company looking for printing services. We sent over three printers to make their *presentations.* The company called us back to tell us that, of the three companies we sent over, they picked one, but that one of the other presenters gave the worst *presentation* they had ever seen. The buyer said that the representative from that company showed up in dirty clothing, a t-shirt, jeans with printing ink on them and wearing torn tennis shoes. On top of that, he smelled as if he hadn't taken a shower in four days.

When we called that printer back to hear his side, he said: *"I don't understand why they didn't pick my company."* The problem here was simple. This printer felt that all he had to do was show up and take the order if someone needed a printing job. He had absolutely no understanding or idea of what it means to give a *presentation.* He was the owner, and while he may have known everything about the printing process, he knew nothing about giving a *presentation* to a prospective buyer or how to even present himself.

While you might think that is just one case of not knowing what to do, think again. I have been in a situation where I was one of three or four presenters sitting in the lobby each waiting to go in and give our *presentation.* While sitting there, I am sizing up my competition. Many times I knew I would get the job just based on how I presented myself as compared to how my so-called *competition* looked. On the other side, I have had people come to my business to give a *presentation* for products that I needed to buy and they were dead when they walked in the door. Dressed in backroom work clothing (which reads, *small company and this is the person doing the work*) and would give me one of those dead fish handshakes. Hiring a company in which the owner gives the *presentation* is fine. But that owner cannot give a *presentation* looking like an hourly employee from the backroom.

It is very important for you to realize that in business, *it can be a cruel world out there*. One mistake can cost you thousands of dollars in lost sales. Some companies are power machines when it comes to giving *presentations* and generating sales. Others, well the owners usually just give up and go back to a 9-5 job, working for someone else because they just never mastered *prospecting, presentation* and *close*.

# The Proverbial "I"

If you are a small one- or two-person business, never make a *presentation* and say *"I."* If you say, *"I can deliver -----,"* *"I can get -----,"* *"I can do this"*, or any other *"I"* you are saying you're a one-person business. Always say, *"our company [we] can deliver -----,"* *"our company [we] can get -----,"* or *"our company [we] can do this -----."* Never say *"I."*

# Never Make Assumptions

A very important point to repeat is that you must never make an assumption about a prospective buyer. That means that you must have a broad understanding of the living and social habits of today's prospects and how they play into society. Prior to the mid-sixtys, young people lived together after they were married, not before. Although there were single moms raising children, they were far and few between. Today, however, it is a different story. Teenagers graduating from high school already have children that they are raising. Young people are living together, raising children, and have no intentions of marriage. Far too many grandparents are stuck raising a small child because their son or daughter brought a child into this world long before they were ready to take on that responsibility. Couples in their mid-thirties are getting married and just starting families. Many older men are getting divorced and marrying women half their age and becoming fathers (parents) all over again. Gay/lesbian individuals and couples are coming out of the closet and some are adopting children. What does all of this have to do with owning a business and selling something? The answer is *simple.*

Never assume that.
- The couple is married,
- The child is their grandchild,
- The customer is a grandfather with his daughter and grandchild,
- The customer is a mother with her 24 year old son,
- She has a husband or he has wife, and
- They are sisters.

The wrong statement, one that could embarrass you or your prospect, could cause you to lose a sale. Never assume anything about your prospects.

# Your *Presentation*

In time you will come to realize that your *presentation* is a unique part of who you are and how your business can or cannot grow. Work hard at developing a good strong *core* to your *presentation*. This is the part that defines you, your company and your products or services. You cannot have a *core* opening as every time you present, the situation will be different. At 10 a.m. you might be making a *presentation* to one person. At 2 p.m. it might be to a small group, and at 4 p.m. to a large group. For each of those, you will have to adapt your opening comments to meet each type of situation. Thus, you need to know how to start your *presentation* based on each different situation you may come across. Once you have completed your opening remarks, you will then give your *core presentation*, which may have to be adapted to that particular group.

The end of your *presentation* has to be a "home run" as it may be the last words they remember. Making a strong finish, also adapted to that group, is extremely important.

Just like a good stage actor must practice his lines, you need to practice your *presentation* over and over again until you can give it in a very *natural, unstrained* manner. If your *presentation* sounds as if you memorized it, you lose. If you are constantly searching for words, you lose. If you have long pauses or hesitation while you talk, you lose.

Learn how to put *enthusiasm* into your *presentation*. If you talk with a *ho hum* tone, you lose. Enthusiasm can be contagious. If you seem enthusiastic about your product or service, you will find that your prospect may also become enthused with what you have to say. Think of it this way. If I said, *"this ice cream is good"* in a monotone voice, would you feel that I was excited about that ice cream? Probably not. If, however, I said, *"man, oh man, this is the **best** tasting ice cream I have ever had"* and I raised my voice when I said *"best,"* you would most likely feel that I was really please with that ice cream. Thus, how good (or bad) that ice cream may be is not the issue. How pleased I seem to be about its taste was confirmed by my enthusiasm in the way I expressed myself. If you can put that type of enthusiasm into your *presentation*, you will increase your chance of making a sale.

# Anyone Can Talk; Learn How to Speak

The best way that you can improve your *presentation* skills is to join your local chapter of Toastmasters International. I don't care if you have been in sales for 30 years, everyone who joins Toastmasters gets something of value out of it, especially when it comes to your *presentation* skills.

Many times when people give *presentations* they have a tendency to talk real fast so that they can get everything in. All that does is make you come across as being nervous. Toastmasters will teach you how to speak professionally and come across the way you want in your *presentation*. I joined Toastmasters International many years ago because I wanted to improve my sales *presentations.* What I learned and put into my *presentations* helped my sales efforts ten-fold. There is absolutely no doubt in my mind that what I learned in Toastmasters contributed greatly to my *presentation* skills and the growth of my companies. Find your local chapter of Toastmasters International and join it.

"If you cannot *close* your sale, you need to hire a closer to *close* the sales for you."

Jerry X Shea

# Chapter 7

## The Close

You have worked hard to find a prospective buyer for your company's products. Assume that you are now with the buyer of that company and have just completed your *presentation*. In your mind, you just gave one of your best *presentations* and it was right on the money. You feel good about your *presentation* and now it is time to *go for the close* and ask for the sale.

As I said at the start of this book, you have to master three things, *prospecting, presentation* and *close.* Fail in any one of these areas and you will not get a sale. I have known many people who can track down prospective buyers better than anyone else, but they cannot make a *presentation.* I have also known people that can't seem to track down anyone who may want or need their product. But if you give them the lead and let them go make their *presentation* they will come back with the sale. Then, there are people that can find the prospect, make a killer *presentation,* but fall flat when it comes to closing the sale. If for any reason, you feel you cannot *close* a sale, you need to find someone that can *close* the sale and pay them a commission for getting the business.

# How Do You *Close* the Sale?

Every time I give my *Prospecting - Presentation - Close* workshop, I always get the most questions on the part of how to *close* the sale. Everyone wants to know *what do I say when I am closing the sale.* But here is the hard part. It doesn't matter what I say. I am not the one giving your *presentation* and trying to *close* your prospect. The big question is, "how do *you close* your sale?"

First, let's understand that there is *no one thing to say that will ever close a sale.* In time, you will find out that you don't even give the same *presentation* every time you present. That is because each and every time you present, the situation will be different. The same goes for closing the sale. No two closings will be the same.

Selling, if you have never done it before, requires a real learning curve before you even get close to being good at it. Large companies spend millions of dollars teaching and training their sales staffs on the techniques of making a sale. Some companies like IBM have month-long courses, with sales internships for additional months, before they ever cut someone loose to go out and sell on his or her own. There are many courses that you can take on selling techniques. I highly recommend you take some courses if you have never sold anything before. For now, however, here are a few things that can help you with your *presentation* and *close*.

# Killing the Sale

You have given your *presentation.* You are getting ready to go for the *close* when you discover the following:

- You just gave your *presentation* to a recommender, not the final decision maker. Thus, you cannot ask for the sale.

This is a real killer. The problem is simple. You should have done a great job of selling yourself. If you did not do a great job of selling yourself (one in which the recommender will recommend you and your company), you will be lost in the shuffle. The person that sells himself or herself will be the one that gets the job.

- You just finished your *presentation* to the owner of the company. However, his wife is also a partner but could not attend today. You are asked, "Can you come back tomorrow?"

This is called a *one-legged presentation.* If you ever have to give a *presentation* to a husband and wife (or two or more business partners), make sure all are present. If not, re-schedule the appointment for another day. You can never sell to one person if there are two or more people who are required to jointly make the decision.

- You just started your *presentation* when the prospect says: *"Can you hurry up? I have to get to another meeting."*

With that, you should stop your *presentation* and tell the prospect: *"These things can happen, but for you to make the correct decision, you really need to hear what I have to say. Since you have to be someplace else, let's reschedule this presentation for another day."* By doing this you will be acknowledging that you know he/she has to get to another meeting, and, when you meet again, your prospect will be even more receptive to your *presentation*. There will be a sense of guilt for cutting you short the first time.

- You are about to ask for the sale when the prospect takes a phone call and talks for the next five minutes while you just sit there.

It's another deal killer. When the call is over, your prospect's mind will be on the phone call. Your momentum will be lost. You need to regain that momentum by reviewing a few points in your *presentation* and then going for the *close* again.

- His/her secretary comes in and interrupts the meeting. He has to leave the office to go out of the room to talk to someone.

Again, you're dead. The longer he is out of the room, the further away he will mentally be from the memory of your *presentation*. When he returns, give another quick overview of your *presentation,* hitting the highlights, and then go for the *close.*

There are many things that can go wrong when you have a meeting with a prospect that can destroy your chances of writing an order that day. In many cases, based on the prospect having a "bad hair day," it may be best to reschedule your meeting for another day. And what kind of bad hair days can a prospect have?

1. When he woke up this morning, he and his wife discovered that their teenage daughter did not come home last night. They have not heard from her and it is now 2 p.m.
2. Her husband asked for a divorce last night.
3. He just found out his wife has a lover.
4. She just found out her husband has a lover and it's another man.
5. His best friend ran off with his wife.
6. The family dog died last night.
7. Someone smashed into her parked car out in the lot and did not leave a note.
8. He got a ticket for speeding on the way to your meeting.
9. She just found out that her teenage son got his girlfriend pregnant.
10. You remind her of her ex husband, whom she hates.

And the list goes on and on. In time you will have your own list. It is hard to believe that, because of a *happening* outside of your control, you lost a sale that day. Here are a few of the ones that really did happen to me and I will never forget them.

- My prospect (a woman in her 40s) had a *fantasy love affair* with actor Antonio Banderas. (She even had a life size poster of him in her office.) The day we met, she had just found out that he was going out with Melanie Griffith. Her day was ruined, not to mention my sale efforts. When she said to me, *"I can't think straight today,"* that said it all.

- As I walked in and shook hands with my prospect, she informed me that she had just come from the doctor and found out that she has diabetes. She asked to cancel the meeting. What am I going to say? *"No?"*

- At the end of my *presentation* the prospect said: *"Thank you, Mr. Shea, but I will not be buying your products. I am leaving the company this Friday but I will pass this information onto my replacement."*

- The head of the business called me to meet with his son. At the meeting, his son said: *"As you know, Mr. Shea, it was my father who wanted me to meet with you and he is a very sick man. I can't place an order with you because, when he dies, we will be closing the business and selling the land to a developer."*

When these things happen, there is nothing you can do about it. Just move on to your next appointment.

# Pricing

Many of you reading this book may have been *kicked to the curb* by prospects who have said: *"Your competition is selling the product for less."* You most likely came to the conclusion that price is everything in a sale. Let me tell you right now, and you can confirm this by just talking to any other seasoned sales person, *price is not the issue.*

Many times when I had my screen printing and embroidery business, I had customers come to pick up their shirts for an event and tell me: "*Jerry, your prices are the highest in the area, but I come here because your service is excellent. We always get our shirts on time and the printing [embroidery] is top quality.*"

What makes a company or person willing to pay more for a product or service? The answer is easy. In most cases, it is because the person is disappointed in the product he or she purchased by shopping for price the first time out. And as the saying goes, *"you get what you pay for."* In my case, many of my customers went to my "so called" competition first. Imagine how they felt when they got the lowest price in town, but when they went to pick up the shirts for their kids' soccer team, they were told: "*Sorry, they are not ready yet.*" What do you think would happen when a company sends someone over to get their t-shirts for the annual company picnic this weekend and they are told that the shirts will be ready next Tuesday? In the eight years that I ran that screen printing company, we never missed a deadline. *Never.* Part of my *presentation* to any company, team, school, etc. was very simple. *"If we don't deliver the job on time, it is free."* While my pricing may have been a little higher than my competition, my guarantee of quality work delivered on time was an easy sell, especially if they tried to get the lowest price the first time only to be told the job was not ready.

Five years after I sold that business, my wife and I purchased the local coffee/espresso shop in a small tourist town. We had to compete with six other coffee/espresso shops within a mile and a half. Our prices for all coffee drinks were higher than any other shop and we had the best business. Why, because we exceeded our customer's expectations. First, we roasted our own beans which made our coffee the freshest in town. Then, we gave the customers just a little bit more whip cream on top of their mochas. When we made an ice blended drink, we put chocolate syrup down the sides of the clear empty cup before we poured in the drink. We added a lot of chocolate on top of our home-made whipping cream. When we presented that drink to a new customer, we always got a *"Wow."* That little extra that went into each drink justified the higher price. It was a simple case of exceeding customer's expectations.

When you are told (after making your *presentation* and going for the *close)*, *"we have a lower price from another company,"* you have to get that prospect's focus off of price. Focus, instead, onto your company's ability to deliver on time and on your use of top quality products or ingredients. Talk about the fact that you are a legal business that pays taxes and does not pay employees under the table. Sell quality not price.

# Scenario #3

You start your *presentation*. The prospect cuts you off and says: *"Let's cut to the chase. What's your price?"* (This can happen many times in your sales carrier.) Your response should be a small laugh as you shake your head left to right (indicating a "no"). Then you say: *"Mr ./ Ms._____, price is not the issue (shake your head again). If you are inter-viewing companies based only on the price of their prod-uct, then as the saying goes 'you'll get what you pay for.' At [your company] we don't sell price. We sell a competitively priced product that is backed by our company and delivered on time. I am willing to give you a great price for our prod-uct; however, we cannot function as a company if we end up in a 'give away' situation with our products. I am sure your company functions that same way. Tell me the price you are looking for and let's see if we can do business together?"*

There is another old saying: *"He who throws out the first figure loses."* What you have done here is to temporarily delay answering the question, *"what's your price?"* so that you are not the first one to *"throw out a price."* You are mak-ing your prospect *"throw out that first price."* Remember, the reason you are there is because the prospect needs to buy the type of product/service you are selling. The problem is that he/she could care less about your company, or any com-pany that can provide the same product/service. They really are trying to make a buy based on price. All this really rep-resents is the start of negotiations and you better be a good negotiator (more on that later).

# Scenario #4
# (Large Volume Sale)

Using the example above, let's assume that your bottom line is $3.62 for each item and that your prospect is buying 10,000 items. Your prospect says: *"We are looking for a price of $3.70."* Since the prospect gave a price above your lowest price, your response should be to look the prospect right in the eye and say: *"Mr./Ms_____, if I sell our product to you at $3.70 each, can I write that order right now?"* Of course, you would try and say that without a great big smile on your face. What is important here is that the price offered by your prospect is what you will accept. You need to leave that office with a written order *NOW.* If you leave without the order, the next person in the door could offer a lower price and you would lose the order.

The other side of that coin, of course, would be that your lowest price is $3.62 and the prospect says: *"We are looking for a price of $3.50."*

# Negotiating

If the prospect gave the lower price ($3.50 in the above example), one that is just too low for your company to be able to make a profit, you have to negotiate for a higher price. Start by saying: *"Mr./Ms._____, if our company could stay in business selling the product at $3.50 each, I would be happy to write that order. But that price is just too low and unrealistic."* (Yes, use the word "unrealistic.") That is because your lowest price is $3.62, but DON'T TELL HIM THAT. When you negotiate, you never throw out your bottom line price up front. You would come back with: *"Our listed selling price is $3.85. How close to the $3.85 price do you think your company could come?"* At this point you are 35 cents apart. You are trying to get to anything above $3.62

(your lowest price). Let's say the prospect says: *"We could go to $3.65"* Obviously, you would say: *"Mr./Ms._____, if I sell you our product at $3.65 each, can I write that order right now?"*

If the prospect came back with a price of $3.58 each, you would now be only 4 cents apart from your very bottom price. Your response would be (shaking your head *no* but not saying the word *no*), *"Mr./Ms._____, with our price being $3.85 each, if I sell them to you for $3.64 each, could we make a deal right now?"* As you say that, look him right in the eye and don't *blink*. Don't say another word. You have just asked for the sale at $3.64 each. Another old cliché in the sales industry is, when a price has been put on the table, *"he who speaks first loses."* If he says *"it's a deal,"* you have just negotiated a price 2 cents above your lowest price. While you might think 2 cents more is hardly anything to rave about, keep in mind that the order is for 10,000 pieces. That is $200 more into your company than if you sold them for your very bottom price.

If your prospect had said *"no"* to the $3.64 price, you still have 2 cents more with which to work. Hopefully, the two of you will end up negotiating to your lowest price of $3.62. If he wants a price of $3.60, you have to make the call of whether to lose the order and hold firm on your $3.62 price (be willing to *walk* if you can't get it) or to accept the prospect's price. Remember, selling below your profit margin will just put you *out-of-business* eventually.

For those of you trying to sell just twelve items at $10 each, the exact same principles of negotiation come into play. If $10 is your lowest price, don't put it out there at the front end. Start at $15 each and negotiate down.

Once, while I was giving a sales seminar I had a guy ask: *"Why not give them your lowest price right up front?"* The answer is easy. If you say *"my price is $10 each,"* your prospect is going to say: *"I am looking for a price of $8 each."* Now what will you do?

You need to remember that there are a lot of people out there who negotiate prices all day long. They also will never give the actual price they are willing to pay for the item right up front either.

# Scenario #5

You have completed your *presentation* and the prospect says: *"Well, that is nice information on your company, but what is your price?"* Again, you start with *"Mr./Ms. _____, our pricing is very competitive., What is your company's budget for this project?"* Remember, he who throws out the first price loses. If the prospect gives a price above your lowest price, you would say: *"Mr./Ms, _____, if I sell you our product at [the price he gave you] each, can I write that order right now?"* If he gives you a price lower than your lowest price, you negotiate as outlined above.

# Scenario #6

The prospect tells you that he has interviewed another company and its price is $ _____. The price is much lower than what your price is (which you have not told him yet). Your reaction should be as follows:

First, act surprised. Drop your mouth open (yes, I really mean that). Shake your head side-to-side in a big way and say: "*No, no, no. Something is wrong with that price. No one can run a company and sell this product at that price. Something is wrong here.*"

Now here are some of the *wrongs* with the price he gave you:

- First, he is lying. He has not talked with any other supplier and is just trying to see if he can get a great low price deal from you.
- Second, the price he gave you *is not* the real price the other company gave him. He is lying on this one also. He is just trying to see if you would go lower than the other company price so he told you a real low price.
- You know for a fact that no one that runs a legitimate business could produce the product at that low a price. (A company, however, that runs an illegal *sweat shop* of underage and undocumented workers probably could produce the product at that price. But you can't.)

So what do you do in a case like this? For the first two, you just have to sell the prospect on your company's capabilities to produce and deliver the product. It will require your own selling technique. Just remember, you are not only selling your company product, you are also selling yourself. Win the prospect over by becoming the type of person with whom the prospect would like to establish a working relationship. Yes, you may have to negotiate price, but that goes with the territory of sales.

Sometimes a prospect will show you the price on an order form from another company. If you know the company (which you should know all of your competitors), and you really feel that they have a price better than you, you may have to review your price structure. Maybe you are the one out-of-line on pricing your products.

Years ago, I put a bid in for a county contract. When they opened all the bids, my company had the second lowest of eleven bids. Two things happened. First, the company that won the bid had prices just too low to make a profit. I knew the profit margins and I knew that they could not do the job at the price they gave and still make a profit. They ended up going *out-of-business* a year later. What was really surprising was that the person who had the eleventh bid (the highest bid of all), had prices that went way over the top. She was not even close to the prices the bottom three had (excluding the winning bid). What she learned was that her pricing structure was so out-of-line that she would never win a bid at her high prices.

If you go out and make *presentations,* and then are told that *"other companies have much lower prices,"* you may very well be the company that is out-of-line in competitive bidding and pricing.

The more you go out and bid on jobs the better you will become at assessing just what it is that these buyers are looking for in price. Buyers set budgets for the projects they are working on and know the price range they need to work in.

One thing you will discover very quickly is that some of the buyers for large companies have been purchasing goods for many years, and they really do know what the price should be for most of the items they purchase. On the other side of the coin, however, you will come across prospects (buyers) that have never purchased what it is that you have to sell. Thus, they don't know the price range of your products/service. One of two things will happen when you come across this type of situation. First, if it is a very experienced buyer, he or she will know enough to get at least three bids for the job. In this case you really do have to know the market for what you are selling. The second type of buyer may have a price range to work in and if you price is in that range they will just go with your price and make the purchase. In time you will find that depending on what you are selling and the experience of your buyer, knowing how to give a good competitive bid for your product/service will result in you *closing* the deal just about every time.

Many times, there is just no real rhyme or reason as to why some people say "yes" to a sale, and others say "no." But, there is one thing for certain. If you don't try your best to sell yourself and your company every time you meet with a prospect and do your best to *close* the sale, you will never create enough sales to stay in business, let alone grow that business.

By how much can you lose or win a sale? Would you believe this one? A buyer purchased a car and paid more for it from a dealer located in another city because she enjoyed the longer scenic drive to get to the dealership and the nice drive back in her new car. To her, price was not the issue.

"Fulfill the customer's needs and you will find the sale."

Jerry X Shea

# *Chapter 8*

## Needs Satisfaction Selling

If you don't understand just what it is that the customer wants or needs, your success in sales will be limited. This goes from automobile sales, appliance sales, insurance sales or home improvement sales. Enter *needs satisfaction selling.* While this form of sales has been around for a very long time, I am always amazed at the organizations, especially automotive dealerships and appliance stores, that don't train their sales staff in *needs satisfaction selling.* Simply put, if a customer has a need (a new car, kitchen stove, life insurance, roof on the house, etc.) and you can identify that need, you will create a sale if you help them find a solution to fix or meet that need.

# The Car Salesperson

For many people, going to the dentist and having a tooth pulled without novocaine is more fun than going to a car dealership to purchase a car. Automobile sales people have been getting a bum rap as "slime ball sales people" for years. While there may have been a time in which a car salesman smoked a big cigar and wore a plaid polyester sport jacket, those days are long gone. Many automobile salespeople, both men and women, support their families as salespersons selling automobiles. You may not realize it, but a good car salesperson can make a very good living selling cars. The key, of course, is to be a *good car salesperson* who truly understands the customer's needs for a car. If you do not understand those needs, you will fail as a salesperson. Thus, *needs satisfaction selling* is a must if you are in the business of selling cars.

# Scenario #7

A husband and wife walk onto a car lot looking for a used car. The salesperson approaches them and says: *"Hi, can I help you?"* The husband says: *"We are looking for a car for my wife."* The salesperson says: *"We have a number of fine choices over there. Go take a look and if you see something you like, I will be happy to take you for a test drive."* The couple walks toward the used cars. Fifteen minutes later the salesperson walks back outside and discovers the couple left the lot. What happened here is simple. The salesperson had an opportunity to help this couple find the car they needed, but he did not know how to implement *needs satisfaction selling.* He had hoped (like that of so many untrained salespeople) that the couple would come back to him and say: *"We are interested in that car over there."* But it didn't happen.

# Scenario #8

The same couple now goes down the street to another dealership and is approached by their salesperson, John. *"Hi. My name is John* (as he hands them his business card) *and welcome to ABC Motors. What kind of a car are you looking for today?"* The husband says: *"Hi John, we are Tom and Sue and we are looking for a car for my wife."* The salesperson says: *"We have a number of fine used cars, Tom and Sue, and each comes with an extended warranty. But let me ask you, Sue, will you use this car for business or for family?"* The salesperson here is establishing whether they are looking for a soccer mom car or a professional car perhaps to be used in real estate sales. Then Sue says: *"I own a small coffee shop and need something with a lot of storage space, but I also need room for taking our kids to school."* With that answer the salesperson knows that he is not going to show them a two seat sport car. He continues addressing the wife as he starts walking towards the used car lot (don't worry, they will follow him). *"So both storage space along with adequate seating is important to you, is that right Sue?"* Sue says, *"yes."* What the salesperson is doing here is to make sure that the couple knows that he has heard what they are looking for and he understands their need for space. The salesperson then says: *"Is there anything else that is important to you in your new car?"* Sue says: *"I have a bad back so the driver's seat really needs to be comfortable. I would also like a nice sound system."*

Because this salesperson has been trained to ask open ended questions of prospective buyers to help him identify the right type of car to show them, in less than one minute he has established what it is they are looking for and can direct them to the right car. Compare that with the other salesperson that just pointed to the used car lot and walked back inside hoping for a sale, John is on his way to creating a sale.

John asks: *"What type of a price range are we working in?"* This is a very important question. You don't want to show a prospective customer a $60,000 car when he or she can only afford a $30,000 purchase. At the same time, you don't want to show them a $15,000 car if they have a budget for a $30,000 car.

Based on their needs and budget, John shows Tom and Sue two mini-vans and an SUV. Each time Sue gets behind the wheel of the car John says: *"How does that seat feel?"* After looking and sitting in the mini vans, Sue falls in love with the SUV. It has an 8-way seat for her comfort, a great sounding stereo with Sirius/XM radio, and the back seats fold down to transport her items for the coffee shop, while still easy to put up for her kids. But John's *needs satisfaction selling* does not stop here. While on the test drive, John points out all the safety features that the SUV has. He even asks Sue to pull into an empty parking lot and make a u-turn and park the SUV to show her its ease in handling. When they get back to the lot, he pops the hood to point out front-end safety features, highlights about the engine and shows them the side impact features. End result, Tom and Sue have just been convinced that this *is* the SUV for them. John has made a sale thanks to his listening skills, problem solving and needs satisfaction selling techniques.

# The Appliance Sale

*Needs satisfaction selling* is for every type of sale. Let's have another couple walk into an appliance store.

# Scenario #9

Bill and Alice walk into an appliance store looking for a new stove for their soon to be remodeled kitchen. The sales-person that greets them is Jack, a *needs satisfaction sales* trained person. Jack introduces himself by saying: *"Hi, I'm Jack* (as he hands them his card) *and you are?"* They tell him *"Bill and Alice."* Jack says: *"And what type of appli-ance are you looking for today?"* Bill says, *"a new stove top."* Jack responds: *"And who is the cook in the family?"* Without that question, many salespeople would start look-ing at the wife as the cook. Jack finds his answer when Bill responds: *"I'm the cook, my wife hates to cook."* Jack says, *"simple foods to eat or more of a gourmet cook?"* Bill says with a laugh, *"I don't know about the gourmet part but definitely more than TV dinners."* Jack says: *"Let me show you our modern day 6-burner stove tops."* Bill says: *"I hadn't really thought about that, but let's take a look."* Jack shows Bill and Alice a number of 6-burner stoves and Bill just can't get over how great the 6-burner Wolf stove top with the thick grates looks. Jack also explains to Bill how a warming-tray would help keep his cooked food hot without over-cooking it when he prepares a large meal. Bill and Alice purchase the 6-burner stop top and the warming-tray.

Just think of what would have happened if another salesperson had waited on them and just pointed to the store area that the stove tops are located.

*Needs satisfaction selling* is so easy if you put the energy into it. Asking questions identifies the customer's needs. You then fill that need and create a sale. It is really that simple.

# What Does the Customer Really Want?

From car sales, kitchen appliances, home improvements, services, insurance or birthday gifts, the principles are the same. What does the customer really want when he walks into your store? The answer is easy. Customers want respect. If you, or your staff, displays a *who cares* attitude, many folks will just turn around and walk right out of the door. Customers are just like you when you are a customer at someone else's store. Sure, you are there to make a purchase. But you want respect for the fact that you are about to give them your hard earned money. The same thing applies when customers come into your store. Treated them with a *matter-of-fact* attitude and you can end up losing the sale.

*" 'Would you like fries with that?'* has to be the greatest add-on sales statement ever created."

Jerry X Shea

# *Chapter 9*

## Common Problems
## in Retail Sales

*What "kills" a retail sale anyway?* The answer to that question is so varied that it would take 28 volumes of a sales encyclopedia to try to answer it (and it would still not cover every downfall). So why don't we look at some of the more common mistakes that are made in a retail sales setting.

When we say "retail" we are talking about a business in which, once the sale has been made, it is the end of the road (as far as any other money exchanging hands) for that item. While many stores may claim to be "wholesale" or "discount" stores, the simple fact is that they are really retail stores. Once you purchase the item, you become the final end-user for that product. From an apple to eat, to a bottle of Zinfandel wine to drink, when you buy it, you are the end-user. There will be no more sales on that item. (Remember, the grower sells his apples to the wholesaler who sells it to the distributor who sells it to the marketer who finally sells it to you.)

When you have a retail store, your goal is to sell as many items as you can (referred to as moving or turning inventory) as quickly as you can. If, at the end of a month, you still have inventory left that you purchased the month before, you are not making much money and will also not have the money to purchase other items for the future. This is especially true if you need to purchase holiday-related items for your store.

One of the biggest problems with a small retail store, and I do mean *biggest problem*, is that the owners/managers hire young minimum wage employees (often just teenagers) that know nothing about sales. You must remember, you own a retail *sales* store. The key word here is *sales.* No sales, no money. It is that simple. So it really begs the question: "Why would someone that owns a business dependent on making sales hire teenagers, who don't have any sales experience, and put them behind the cash register?" Step back for a second and take a good look at that. Tell me *why?* The answer of course is simple. *"We can't afford to pay for a real salesperson. We are just a small gift shop."* My answer to that is very simple. *"You can't afford not to have a good salesperson."* Well, hang on because I have good news. You can afford good salespeople and they are called *senior citizens.*

Do you realize how many people spent their working life in sales and are now retired? They would love to have a place to go to for a few hours a day, a couple of days a week (not to mention a little extra cash). Here are people that know more about sales than you may ever know and they would love to go to work for you. Think about it.

While you think about it, think of this. The other reason small retail businesses may fail is that many times the owners themselves have never had sales training. Thus, even they don't know how to really sell to a customer.

# "Would You Like Fries With That?"

When you walk into a McDonald's fast food restaurant and have every intention of ordering just a hamburger, what happens when you get up to the counter? The person behind the counter (which may indeed be a teenager, but has had some sales training) says: *"Would you like fries with that?"* Even though you intended to only buy a hamburger, what do you say? You say, *"sure."* What has just happened is called an add on, bump or up-sale. The counter person has just taken a customer who intended on spending one amount of money and got them to increase that amount (which, of course, increases the profits for the company).

So why don't small retail gift shops do the same? Simple, they don't make french fries. OK, so that is a cheap shot, but do you get the message? When you ask a customer if he wants or need something else, you may be surprised when he answers *"yes."* But the customer will never say *"yes"* if you don't ask him or her. Check out this next scenario.

# Scenario #10 –
# The Gift Shop

You own a small gift shop. Your teenage employee is behind the cash register. She is texting her friend on her cell phone when a customer walks in. Big deal, she just keeps texting her friend. The customer walks up to the cash register with a designer salad bowl. Ms. teenager puts down her cell phone, takes the salad bowl from the customer, looks at the price and punches in $19.99 on the cash register (which automatically adds the tax). She says, *"that will be $21.39."* She takes $25 from the customer and, handing her the change, says *"thank you."* The customer leaves and the teenage salesperson returns to texting her friend. Your store just took in $19.95 in a sale.

# Scenario #11 –
# The Gift Shop

Same store as above only a real salesperson is behind the cash register. When the customer comes in, she says *"welcome to Ideal Gifts."* The customer looks around and walks up to the cash register with a $19.99 salad bowl. The salesperson says: *"Oh, I just love that salad bowl. It makes such a perfect gift."* Let's *stop* here for a second. When was the last time you went out and purchased a salad bowl in a gift shop for your own use? Does *seldom* come to mind? The key here is that the salesperson suspects that the customer is not buying that salad bowl for herself, but that it may be a gift for someone else. So she is prepping the customer for an up-sell.

The customer says: *"Yes, I am getting it for a friend's birthday."* The sales person says (very enthusiastically): *"You know what goes great with that salad bowl are these designer salad tossing forks"* (as she walks from behind the cash register over to the salad tossing forks). She shows them to the customer, and the customer agrees that they do go with the salad bowl and says: *"OK, include those."* This is the equivalent of *"do you want fries with that?"* The salesperson says: *"Would you like me to gift wrap it?"* The customer says: *"That would be great."* While wrapping the gift, the salesperson says: *"Do you have a card to go with this? We have a great selection of cards right over there. Go take a look while I wrap this."* When the gift is all wrapped, the customer returns with a card (this is the equivalent of another *"do you want fries with that?")* to go with the gift. She shows the customer the gift wrapped package, and with a smile on her face and in her voice she says: "*Will there be anything else for you today?"* (Sometimes to your surprise the customer may see something else and also buy it.) When the salesperson rings up the order it is now for the salad bowl at $19.99, the fork set at $9.99, and the card at $2.50 – a total of $32.48, plus tax. The customer leaves the store knowing that she has just done *one-stop shopping*, the gift (wrapped) and the card all in one stop. The customer is happy and your store just made an additional $12.49 on that one sale. That is a 62% increase over the original purchased item (that the teenager sold). Just image how much greater your business would be if, every time you rang up a sale, you had that *"do you want fries with that?"* added on to the sale? Better put, if you had a small gift shop that grossed about $250,000 a year, and you could *"add fries"* to each sale, you could turn that into a $405,000 business. While every sale will not increase by 62%, just a 5% increase (because of what a salesperson may say compared to the teenager) could mean the difference between just making it in business and having a great year.

One of the major reasons small businesses fail is because the owners and the people working in the stores do not have sales experience. How many times have I heard someone say: *"I don't want to be pushy and try to sell someone something."* What he or she doesn't understand is that being in sales does not mean that you have to be *pushy*. It just means that you need to learn how to sell without being *pushy*.

As I pointed out in Chapter 6, you must become a problem solver. What is the customer's problem? She needs a gift for a friend. So help her find everything she needs for that gift. Solve the problem of finding a gift and you will increase your sales. Unfortunately, small business owners that do not know how to sell to people may be forced, at some point, to put a sign in their window that says *"going out-of-business."*

This would be a good time to point out the importance of being able to talk to customers who walk into your store. To illustrate this, let's talk about *you* going into a department store to buy a shirt. Now I want you to think this through with me. You walk into the department store and head over to the shirt section. As you enter the area a salesperson says: *"Hi, can I help you?"* Now think for a second on this. What do *you* and the majority of people say when asked *"can I help you?"* You know the answer, it's: *"No, I'm just look-ing."* Now why do *you* and just about everyone else answer with *"no, I'm just looking"* when you know for a fact that you have gone to that store to buy a shirt? That answer is also easy. *We are just conditioned to give that answer.* For many, in less than 30 seconds after being asked if they could use some help and having said *"no,"* they will turn right around and ask the salesperson: *"Do you have a shirt in size _____ ?"* What has happened is that you (or any customer) have come to the point where you need help in finding what you want. So you now ask for that help. But most customers, upon entering a store, do not want immediate help.

Now let's get back to your store. A customer comes in and you say: *"Can I help you?"* The customer says: *"No, I'm just looking."* So do you say anything or do you just let him or her look around? A good sales person will still respond to the *"no, I'm just looking"* comment. I once worked in a high-end wine shop for a while and, on slow days, when customers came into the store, instead of say-ing *"can I help you?,"* I would say, with a smile on my face and in my voice, *"welcome to the best 'just looking' store in town."* Most people would laugh and it was amazing how it helped to establish a rapport with them. Every time I was on a shift, I *worked* each and every customer and the store sales increased. The owner was so pleased that she started giving me a bonus on each sale I made. Here I was just working to have something to do but, because of my sales experience, the owner was having an increase in overall sales.

Right now while writing this part of the book, I am in Alaska on a four-month motorhome trip. We are in the town of Skagway. While walking the town, we noticed that just about every gift shop had retired senior citizens that came up to Alaska for the summer to work in the stores. Their enthusiasm and conversation with everyone that came in helped create a real fun and enjoyable atmosphere. Unfortunately, most often you will just not get that type of environment in a store with teenagers that only have an interest in texting their friends all day long. Please understand that I am not saying that you should never hire teenagers. Some teenagers are very outgoing and do a great job of communicating with prospective customers (buyers). When you find one, hire him or her. You will also find many young adults, in their early 20s, who want summer jobs. Some are very outgoing and will talk and work with customers. One of the stores we went into here in Skagway had such a fellow. You would think that he was the happiest guy in town. He was talking it up with every customer who came up to his cash register and just seemed to be having wonderful time. And yes, he was doing a great job of asking customers if they wanted anything else (*"fries with that?"*). When we went back to that store the next day, there he was, just as outgoing as the day before. That is an employee that will ring up far greater sales (dollar-wise) than the gum chewing, text messaging teenager that just sits behind the counter waiting for someone to walk up and say, *"I'll take this."* It is your store. If you want success, hire real salespeople and start selling those fries.

In Chapter 6, I explained the difference between open-ended questions and closed-end questions. Go to that Chapter and review that section. It also applies to retail sales.

# Two Different Discounts

As we ended our trip to Alaska, we had two different types of sales experiences. Both are worth mentioning. On what is called the inside passage is a town called Ketchikan, the last stop. It was also two weeks until the end of the tourist season. The large cruise ships would no longer be bringing thousands of tourists to any of the towns in Alaska after the end of September. (The next season would start in April.) As a result, all of the tourist retail stores will close up shop in two more weeks until next year. What we found interesting was that with six or eight retail stores on each side of the street, close to half of them were jewelry stores. I never saw so many jewelry stores concentrated into one area as I have seen in Skagway, Juneau and again here in Ketchikan.

Because my wife and I would be celebrating our 35th wedding anniversary at the end of the year, we decided to buy new wedding bands. The purchase would also remind us of our four-month trip to Alaska.

Every jewelry store in town has big signs: *"End of Season Sale," "40%-60% Off," "Total Inventory Must Go."* As we walked the town, we took a look in each jewelry store for something that would catch our eye. One store had such rings. We both liked the matching ammolyte rings. The pair of rings was priced at $6,000. The sign said: "40%- 60% Off." Now keep in mind what I said about a discounted price. They are offering 40% - 60% off of *what?* Jewelry is really marked up. Do you think those rings will really sell for $6,000? Of all the retail businesses that are out there, jewelry stores will almost always negotiate their prices. They expect to negotiate.

As we talked with the sales girl, she immediately took out her calculator, punched some buttons and turned the calculator around (this is a *closing* technique) to show us the discounted price of $1,860 for both rings. That would be a 69% discount.

Let's break this down into sales talk. Remember what I also said in Chapter 7 about *"he who throws out the first figure loses."* They had the rings priced at $6,000 (for both), so that was *their first price they threw out.* At this point I did not ask for any discount or give any price that I would be willing to pay for the rings. When she *volunteered* the discounted price of $1,860, that was the second time *she threw out a price.* With signs in every jewelry store all over town saying "40%-60% Off" and her price of 69% off, do you think that was her final price?

Do you also remember in Chapter 7 ("The Close") when I said that you should *never give your true bottom line price that you have to leave room for negotiations?* So, was $1,860 her final price? *Of course, not.* I then countered her price and said: *"If you make the price an even $1,500 we will buy the rings."* That would make it a 75% discount. What do you think happened next?

She brought in the store manager and told him what we had offered. He said: *"What type of credit card will you be putting this on?"* (That statement is another *closing* technique). By asking for my credit card, he had agreed to the $1,500 price. Do you think the store lost money on that transaction? Of course, not. They know what they really paid for the rings and were willing to take a little less, yet make a sale.

In contrast to that, I wanted to buy two knives from a gift store also in Ketchikan. That store had an Alaskan Ulu knife with a decorative handle and a fish filet knife, also with a decorative handle. The store had a sign: *"20% Off of Everything in the Store."* I spoke with the owner. He gave me the full price for both knives and then took 20% off. I offered to buy both knives for a 50% discount. What do you think he did?

While he was willing to give a 20% discount, that 20% was all he was willing to give. He said: *"If I don't sell them in the next two weeks, I will just pack them up and save them for next season."* He knew every store in town was giving end-of-the-season discounts, yet he was only offering 20% and that was it. What do you think I did here?

Remember when I said *"price is not the issue?"* What is the issue here? The issue is I wanted to have those knives for our kitchen. While it is always nice to get any type of discount you can when you buy anything, I would have even paid full price because I really wanted those knives. So yes, I took the 20% off price and bought the knives.

So what is the lesson learned in these two sales? Easy, *price should never be the issue.* You sell your merchandise for whatever price the market will bear. Understand your market, understand your competition and understand how to price your products so they will sell and you will make a great living in retail.

**Bonus hint:** As a business owner, when you negotiate a price, *always let the buyer win.* If a buyer offers a price that is really off the wall (lower than the price you paid for the item), then obviously you are not going to *let the buyer win* the negotiations. If, however, you learn the art of negotiating and can negotiate a price in the range that you would sell the item, *let the customer win the negotiations*. If you try to continue to negotiate (when the offer is in your acceptable price range), you may see the customer walk right out of your store.

*"I use to get my shirts from another store that had really cheap prices, but they went out-of-business."*

Statement made by a customer to the cashier in my store.

# *Chapter 10*

## What Would You Say
## To The Prospect?

Whatever type of business or sales you are in, you must have a plan for continually *prospecting* for new clients. Your *presentation* and sales skills must be top notch. And, of course, you really do have to know how to *close* the sale.

Read the following different sets of selling/buying examples and think of what you would have said to create or save the sale. There will be times when you can't *close* the sale, and that is to be expected. If, however, you call on ten prospects and can't *close* any of them, something is wrong with your sales approach and closing techniques.

Let's start with a very simple real life sales event. Put yourself in the position of the sales person at an art gallery. After you read the following, come up with your answer before you read on.

# Scenario #12 –
# The Art Sale

My wife and I had just purchased a new house. We had a lot of empty wall space and wanted to put some temporary art work on the walls. We knew that in time we would find the art we really wanted, but for now, we just wanted to fill the empty spaces on the walls. A few days later while driving down a main boulevard in Los Angeles, we saw an advertising sign that read "Art Sale – 40% to 60% Off."

We stopped in and found a number of prints in frames that we liked and thought would fit the temporary need for art on our walls. For each piece that we wanted, we asked the salesperson to please place it off to the side. When we finally had a number of pieces, we asked him to give us a total price. When he gave us the figure after taking 60% off, I asked for an additional 20% off. Remember, the sign out front said "40% - 60% Off." What would you have done if you were the sales person and I asked for an additional 20% off?

Think out your answer before you read on.

What was the end result? He sold us all of the art work for the additional 20% off. You may ask yourself *why would he do that?* The answer is easy. If he could not have made any money on the sale, he would have said *"no"* to the additional discount. If he felt he needed to get more money, he could have said: *"I can't take another 20% off but I can sell them to you with an additional 10% off."* Would I have said *"no, I won't buy the art?"* Of course, not. I still would have made the purchase even if he had said no more discounts. His sale of 40%-60% off always begs the question - *40% to 60% off of what?* A price that has already been marked up 10 times? A price that was so over the top that none of his art was selling? Your lesson here is for you to realize that you will find many buyers asking for an additional discount, no matter what you are selling. That does not mean you have to give it to them. And if you don't, it doesn't mean that they will not buy from you. It is called *negotiations* and you better know how to do it. Getting upset when a buyer wants an additional discount from you will never create a sale.

# Scenario #13 – Selling a Service

Let's say that you are selling a service such as carpet cleaning. You go to a house and work up an estimate. You present your price to the customer and she says: *"Do you have a senior discount?"* Well, do you? Or, do you say: *"Our prices are the same for everyone."* The customer then says: *"The price is too high. I need to get another estimate"* (from another carpet cleaner). What do you say here?

Think out your answer before reading on.

What we have here is someone who just wants a lower price. It may not have made any difference what price you gave, she would have still asked for a senior discount or lower price. So what do you do? Any good salesperson would try to find out just what price she is willing to pay and get a contract to do the work right now, if that price is acceptable to you. If you leave and let her call in another carpet cleaner, it will not matter what price that other company gives, that company will most likely end up getting the job. The buyer will be too embarrassed to call you back. If someone wants your service, your job is to get the contract *now*. You may not get a second chance with that buyer if you don't *close* the sale right now. Say to the prospect: *"Ms. _____, let's see if I can save you the time and trouble of finding someone else to try and get a lower price. What price are you looking for?"* If her price is not that far off, then give it to her and *close* the deal. If you gave it to her for $25 dollars less, it's no big deal. You got the job. *Close* the sale by agreeing to her price (if you can still make a profit) and move on to the next prospect.

# Scenario #14 –
# The Retail Sale

Are you thinking of owning a retail gift shop? How would you handle the customer who comes into your shop and wants to buy the special wine holder that you have priced at $79.99. She says: *"Will you take $60?"* What is your answer?

Think out your answer before reading on. There are two types of retail stores. One is the corporate/franchise owned store in which every item has a bar code price tag. The person behind the cash register is just an employee without any authority to lower any price. The marked price is the selling price and that is it.

Your other retail store is found on every main street in America - the *mom and pop* owned retail store. From the store in a small strip mall next to a barber shop to those in the popular tourist towns, you find their prices are either hand written or priced with an old-fashion pricing gun. If you are the owner of a *mom and pop* gift store and someone asked if you would sell your $79.99 wine holder for $60, you need to assess that offer. How many more do you have? If you have a store room full of these wine holders and you bought them over a month ago and, to date, you have not sold one, I would say, *"SOLD for $60."* In business, you cannot have inventory just sitting there. Turning inventory (selling it) is the name of the game. If, however, you purchased 10 wine holders and have sold 9 at the full $79.99 price and this is the last one, there is no reason to lower your price. I would tell the customer: *"I ordered 10, have sold 9 and this is the last one. I have no reason to lower the price on this item."* Or, if you still want to sell it, negotiate the price. Tell the customer: *"I can't sell it for $60 but if you are willing to pay $69.99 I will sell it to you."* The key here is: *what are you willing to sell that item for **today***. Also keep in mind the day and time. If it is Saturday morning on a holiday weekend, why give a discount? On the other hand, assume that it is a slow Wednesday. You have had only a couple of sales for the day and the holiday weekends are over until next month. Maybe a $60 sale is better than no sale. It is your call. It is your business and you better know each and every day just how you intend to handle someone who wants a discount. After all, the world is full of bargain hunters.

When we are talking about creating a sale or going for the *close*, it is extremely important that you understand that there is a big difference between selling one retail item (or providing a service to a single home) compared to volume sales from a manufacturer. A manufacturer does not sell one item at a time and its profit margins (per item) are much different than your one-item retail sale.

## How Would You Answer These Questions From Your Prospect?

You just gave a great *presentation* and have just asked for the sale. Your price is on the table and your prospect says the following:

## 10 FEARED QUESTIONS or STATEMENTS

1.  *"Is that your best price?"*
2.  *"I don't think we can do business, your prices are too high."*
3.  *"Do you have another product line that is less expensive?"*
4.  *"I need to talk to some other suppliers before I commit."*
5.  *"Why is your price so high?"*

6. *"Your price is very low compared to the other bids and that leads me to believe that your product is inferior."*
7. *"Your pricing is fine, but what else can your company offer?"*
8. *"Do you have an 'in' with the local NBA team for good seats?"*
9. *"My brother-in-law back east says your price is too high."*
10. *(My all time favorite) "No – not interested."*

So how would you respond to the above questions or statements? Let's look at each one.

1. *"Is that your best price?"* Well – is it? Remember, you don't give your lowest price up front. That statement is just a set up for negotiations. So –- negotiate.
2. *"I don't think we can do business, your prices are too high."* Have you reached your true bottom line or are your prices out-of-line with y*our competiti*on?
3. *"Do you have another product line that is less expensive?"* Well, do you? Depending on what you are selling, you need to determine if there is another product your company can offer that is basically similar, but cheaper for you to produce. You can then charge a lower price and pass the savings onto your prospect?
4. *"I need to talk to some other suppliers before I commit."* When a prospect says this you need to counter immediately with: *"What is it that you feel another company will offer you that I can't?"* In short, what is it that this prospect needs to hear or find out before

he/she can commit to making a purchase. This is a very important objection that you must overcome before you can move forward.

5.  *"Why is your price so high?"* OK, why *is* your price so high? Or, is your prospect just playing with you to try and get a lower price? Maybe your price is the lowest he has found after looking at three other companies and he is just trying to get you to go even lower. Or, maybe your price is too high. Do you know if your price is too high or just right compared to your competitions' prices? This is one you must really master as you will hear that question many times.

6.  *"Your price is very low compared to the other bids and that leads me to believe that your product is inferior.*

    Oh, this is just great. You gave your bottom line price and it seems that your prospect thinks it is too low. In fact, it is so low you have just lost the negotiations. After all, you cannot go back up in price. So now what do you say? You really need to figure this one out should this happen. And guess what? One day it will happen. If you really did throw out your lowest price first, you don't deserve the job. Remember, *never give your lowest price up front.* If you had started at a higher price and he said *"your price is very low,"* that would be a different thing. Here is a hint: maybe the other companies' prices are really too high and yours is just right. Ask the prospect: *"What are the other prices?"* If they are truly much higher and you can do the job at the price you gave, fight for your price and convince him/her that it is the other companies that are out-of-line and charging too much.

7.  *"Your pricing is fine, but what else can your company offer?"* Watch out for this one. This guy is looking for a free dinner for two at some high-end restaurant at your expense. Unfortunately, there are many prospects/buyers out there that will make a purchase or give a contract to a company that provides *extra service* for them. My advice to you is – walk away and walk fast. This is the type of company/person that in the long run could end up putting your company out-of-business, especially when government officials step in and investigate improper business practices. Don't fall for this one no matter how big the contract may be.

8.  *"Do you have an 'in' with the local NBA team for good seats?"* This is the same as the one above. Stay away from this one, too. If the prospect can't conduct business without getting free tickets to a sporting event, you don't need to do business with this company. Note: If you have been doing business with a company for a long time and want to sponsor a "company night" at some sporting event in which you invite a number of your customers to join you, that is one thing. An individual prospect who you just met who is trying to get tickets to a game is a different situation. Stay away from doing business with him or her.

9.  *"My brother-in-law back east says your price is too high."* This is an easy one. You just tell your prospect that *"prices on the east coast are never the same as the prices on the west coast"* (or whatever state you are in). Tell your prospect that if he/she wants to purchase the product from another state that

he/she should keep in mind that there will be ship-ping charges involved, compared to your *free deliver.*
10. (My all time favorite) After making your *presenta-tion* at a prospect's business, he/she says: *"No – not interested."* Your answer: *"Well thank you for your time, but may I just ask, why am I here if you are not interested in our product(s)?"* See what he/she says and go from there. After all, if someone agreed to meet with you, that person must have had some inter-est in what you are selling. So why is he or she *"not interested"* now? Ask if price is the issue? Maybe he/she thought your item sold for $10 and are shocked to find out that it sells for $100. If that is the case, you did a poor job of *prospecting.* If the prospect really is not interested in what you are selling, take advantage of the moment and ask him/her: *"Do you know of anyone at another company or through your network contacts that could use our product?"* You may be surprised when they give you the name and phone number of a couple of other people for you to contact.

# So Just What Is Your Price Anyway?

For every item that you sell, you must know your bottom line price. To sell that item for just one cent below that bottom line price would be a foolish business decision, especially if you already know you cannot make a living selling the item below that price. If you feel that your competition is beating you on price, you need to step back and re-evaluate your purchasing and production costs. Research everything that you buy and do in order to offer that product for sale.

# Scenario #15 – Sell *Me* Your Product/Service

It is time to put *you* to the test. Here is how it will work. First, you need to do this without any interruptions. Thus, go into a back-room or office. Turn off your cell phone (and the house phone), radio, and TV. Eliminate any other possible distractions. If you are doing this at home with a family, tell everyone not to bother you until you come out of the room. (And keep the dog quiet.) It is very important that you give this your full attention. I need you to mentally prepare yourself as if the success of your business depends on the next 10 minutes. If you can't do this now, do it later.

**The Scenario:** Assume that, because of your great *prospecting,* I have responded and indicated that my company is interested in purchasing what you sell. We are meeting at my office tomorrow at 10 a.m.

**The Set-up:** First, set up a video camera or audio recorder of some type to record your *presentation*. Ask a family members or co-worker to pick three numbers between 1 and 10. Write those numbers down in the order they gave them to you. Now turn on your video camera or audio recorder.

**Your *Presentation*:** Imagine that when you walk into that back-room or office, you are walking into my office. Seated with me are two of my other employees. Enter the room with the video/tape recorder running.

**Key to this Scenario:** Once you walk into the room to give your *presentation,* you cannot stop or start over again if you feel you made a mistake. After all, you cannot start over again in a real life situation. So make this a real situation. Take this book with you. Enter the room and imagine the three of us sitting at a table.

**Ready, set, GO** – Enter the room. Now let's hear your *presentation.*

\* \* \*

Between 5 and 10 minutes later (after you have finished your *presentation*), assume that I say the following; *"Thank you, Mr./Ms._____, I have a question."* Now, remember those numbers your family member gave you that were between 1 and 10? Turn to page 116 in this book, "10 FEARED QUESTIONS or STATEMENTS." Read the first number that your family gave you. That is *my* question (or statement) to you now. Respond by saying out loud: *"Your question (or statement) to me is:_____ (read it)."* Then answer the question or respond to the statement.

When you have finished, look at the next number your family member gave you and match it to the question or statement on page 116. Read it out loud as if one of my employees had just said that to you. Respond to this second one and move on to the final numbered item. Read the last one out loud as if my other employee had just said that to you, and respond accordingly. When you have finished responding to the three questions or statements, consider your *presentation* over.

**How do you think you did?** You can find out by playing back the video or audio tape. The more you "role play" your *presentation,* the better you will become at it. Practice over and over again. At one time I had a sales job in which every week, rain or shine, we had to give our *presentation* in front of the other salespeople, and it was video-taped. Then everyone in the room reviewed it. Since you may not be part of a sales team, you still need to practice as much as you can, as often as you can. If you can't make a great *presentation*, you will never get to the *close.*

While we can't really do a written exercise on closing a sale, you can still practice your closing techniques. Turn on that video camera and go for the *close*. Practice, practice, practice, and then practice some more.

"Lack of follow-up is one of the biggest killers of future sales."

Jerry X Shea

# *Chapter 11*

## The Follow-Up

You are *prospecting* for new clients each and every day. Your *presentation* to those prospects is flawless. When you go for the *close* you do it with confidence and your prospects become clients because they agree to buy from you. Congratulations, you are creating sales. Now what? This is the point in which many salespeople (and many companies) fail. They forget about the *follow-up*. Sure you made the sale, but what about future sales to the same person? Better yet, how about your satisfied customer referring you to a friend or relative?

Here is a great question for you. What is the name of the real estate person who sold you your home or condo? What is the name of the salesperson who sold you your car? If you had a pool or a room added onto your house, what is the name of the contractor? What is the name of your insurance agent? Chances are, you, just like most people, cannot remember the names of those people. You know why? Each of these salespeople most likely did not have a *follow-up* program in place. If they did, you would know their names.

Every time you allow a paying customer to walk away without ever seeing, talking or contacting that person again, you are a *weak* salesperson. You are *weak* because you failed to *follow-up.* It is the biggest down fall of many salespeople and companies.

Think of it this way. Assume that you sold something to 10 people and that each of those 10 told a relative, neighbor or co-worker about you, As a result, assume further that you received just one referral (from each of them). You would have gained 10 more prospects. Just imagine if two or three referrals from each of the 10 people walked through the door asking for you. Referral business is big business for any company or salesperson, yet very few salespeople have a *follow-up* program that helps them get those referrals. But wait, there's more. What about selling to that original customer again in a few years? It will never happen unless you have a *follow-up* program in place.

A good *follow-up* program is so easy and it works like this.

**First:** As soon as the customer walks out of the door with his or her new purchase, you should be sending a thank you card (or e-card). After all, if that person purchased a home, car, insurance or any service from you, you would have his or her name, address, phone number and email address. Just because the sale part is over and you have cash in your pocket is no excuse never to contact that person again. So send out that thank you card (or e-card). (Many card companies have thank you cards for specific industries. Check them out.) For written cards, put a few of your business cards into the envelope, address and stamp the card, and mail it immediately.

(Note: To those of you in your '20s and '30s who are saying to yourself: *"How old-fashioned. No one sends written cards anymore."* If your sale is to someone in their '60s or older, they *are more likely to be old fashioned.* Send the card.)

**Second:** Between three and five days after you made the sale, call the purchaser to make sure everything is fine. In this call, you ask that buyer if he or she has any friends or relatives who could also use your service or product. If the answer is "yes," ask if you could get the name and telephone number of the friend or relative, and if it would it be acceptable for you to contact the person. If not, ask them to pass on your name to the interested friend or relative.

**Third:** Make sure you add your purchaser's name and address to your contact list because, every three or six months, you are going to send a newsletter (see Chapter 4) to everyone on that list.

**Fourth:** Every first week in January (right after New Year's Day), 4th of July, Halloween, Thanksgiving or December Holiday Season (pick one), you will send another card to everyone on your list. Again, check for companies that sell seasonal or holiday cards.

**Fifth:** Mail them a birthday card. You will know their birthdays because you will have asked them the month and day (not year) they were born and have entered it into your data base, didn't you?

What you are doing here is keeping your name and company name in front of your customers' eyes at least five times a year. Don't send emails unless there is a real reason to do so and they have told you that they don't mind receiving emails from you. You never want to send junk mail.

If you send written cards, make sure you sign your name to each holiday card and hand-write each personal birthday card. (Don't stick a print-out statement from your computer on your card.) Remember, a printed sticker with someone's name on it really says "this is junk mail." Many times, it will get thrown out without ever being opened. So the best way to make sure your customer will open the envelope is to hand write his or her name and address. A hand-written envelope is considered "A" mail and is more likely to be opened because it has been personalized to him or her.

Now go find those cards, start that birthday file and get to work on your newsletter. Don't let all your efforts of *prospecting, presentation* and *close* fall by the way side by letting your customer fade off into the fog never to be seen again. Stay in touch with a solid follow-up program.

# Pre-Sales Follow-up

I can't even begin to count the number of times that a salesperson failed to follow-up with me when he knew I was out to buy what he had to sell. To think that a prospective buyer comes to you (you did not have to go *prospecting* to try and find that buyer) and because that buyer did not buy from you today, you never even try to contact him/her again. Now ask yourself this question: *"why should any consumer come back and buy from you when there are hundreds of other salespeople selling the same item at other stores/companies?"* This is especially true in the case of large ticket items, such as kitchen appliances, a new car, boat, RV, or any item in which the first thing the consumer is doing is *"taking a look at what is out there."* Follow-up with any consumer you make contact with who showed an interest in what it is you have to sell is paramount to being successful in sales.

TRUE STORY: My wife and I were looking at an expensive item that we intended to purchase after we sold some property. The salesperson was a young member of a family owned business. We explained right up front that we could not make a purchase today, but once the property sold we would be ready to buy. We were at the point of narrowing down just what it was we would be purchasing when the time comes. This young salesperson said: *"If I was a good salesperson, I would be selling this to you right now."* I reminded him that no matter how good a salesperson he could be, we were not in the financial position to make a purchase at this time. We gave him our names, phone number, mailing address and email address. After we left, we never heard from him again. No email, no phone call, nothing. The person in that business that oversees this young salesperson is doing him and the company a big disservice by not explaining to him how important follow-up is to the success of future sales.

I can think of many times when I made a sale a month, six months or even a year after meeting the prospective customer. This happened because I stayed in touch with the prospective buyer by implementing and executing my follow-up program. If you want to be successful in sales, then lean to follow-up on each and every lead, prospect or sale you make.

Three words that also equal success – "location, location, location."

One of the oldest, yet true, adages of business

# *Chapter 12*

## The Do's and Don'ts of Small Business

While writing *Prospecting – Presentation - Close*, I was reminded in every chapter of this book of some of the very big mistakes I have seen small business owners make over the years. As a realtor selling small business opportunities, and as a small business owner running my own businesses, I want to take a few minutes to look at some of the mistakes I have witnessed over the years. Some of the small business owners I have encountered made mistakes that caused them to not only lose the sale but even their businesses.

## The Take Back

Many times when you are giving your *presentation* (depending on your type of business), you may hand out samples of your work for the prospect to review. If the prospect is inter-viewing a number of potential vendors, you will leave the meeting and let the prospect keep the samples. In this way, the prospect can compare your samples to those of the other companies being interviewed. This is pretty much standard procedure. You have to take into account that part of your *presentation* includes leaving those samples with the poten-tial buyer._

Don't plan on getting your samples back, especially if the prospect decides to go with another company. (This begs the question: What did you do wrong in your *presentation*?)

Image what your chances would be of getting another opportunity to make a *presentation* (maybe next year) if, when told that you did not get the job this time, you demanded that the prospect return your samples? I can't begin to tell you how many times I have spoken (and laughed) with pur-chasing agents about small business owners demanding that the prospects return the samples (especially when the busi-ness owner did not get the job). One time, an owner gave a very expensive desk clock to a prospective client. When the client chose a different company, this small business owner demanded that the prospect return the clock. Why she gave the agent the clock in the first place is beyond me since she was not in the business of selling clocks. The purchasing agent told me that he would never deal with her again. This, of course, is very sad. Maybe she did not get the job this time, but she had an "in." She had met the agent and he gave her an opportunity to make a *presentation*. The next time that purchasing agent interviews prospective vendors, he will most likely not include her.

The lesson learned here is simple. You must take into account that the cost of handing out samples (if that is what you do) must be part of your marketing budget. Asking prospective buyers to return your sample(s) tells the world that you are a "small under-budget" company.

# The Rewards Card

If you have ever gone into a coffee/espresso café, you most likely were exposed to its "rewards card" programs. This card may give the purchaser a free drink or other free add-on when you have purchased the required number of drinks.

When my wife and I owned our espresso shop in Cambria, California, we had a rewards card that the customers loved. Every 10th drink was free. Even the tourists who would come to town only once or twice a year would still bring in their rewards cards to mark their purchases. Then one day, upon another visit to town, the tourist would come in for his or her free drink. With 6 espresso shops within a one and a one-half mile long main street, the rewards card was helpful in getting clients to come back to us.

On the other side of this, there was a coffee/espresso shop down the street from where I had my business 10 years ago. Three days a week I drove to a supplier about 20 minutes away. On those days, I would go out of my way to go to this coffee/espresso shop to get an ice-blended mocha. It was a nice little shop and the owner was a very pleasant woman. I would come in around 2 p.m., a slow time for all coffee shops. Many times, I was the only one in her shop at that time and the owner would always ask me how my day was going. Sometimes we would "talk business" and what was going on in our area.

One day I walked in and a new woman was behind the counter. When I asked about the former owner, she said that the former owner sold the business to her and that she was now the new owner. I shook her hand, congratulated her on her purchase and ordered my drink. As she made my drink, I tried to engage in conversation. All I got back from her was short answers in what seemed like a one-way conversation.

When she brought my drink to the counter, I handed her the money along with my rewards card (which was two punches away from a free drink). She said: *"We don't take these anymore."* And she handed the card back to me. A little shocked, I said: *"This was such a great idea and I go out of my way to come here because of the rewards card."* She said: *"I don't want to take them."* I said: *"I bet there are a lot of these out there and it may hurt your business if you stop honoring them."* She replied: *"Yes, a lot of people come in here with them, but I am not going to do that program."* I said: *"What kind of a rewards program are you going to do?"* She said: *"I don't know yet."* I left with my drink and never went back again. Six months later, I drove by and the place was closed.

The sad lesson learned here is that the previous owner had worked hard to establish a friendly coffee shop and reward her customers for coming into her shop. This new owner spent money to buy a *turn-key* business that was all set up and running. She then undoes the good the original owner worked hard at establishing.

Give the customers a good reason to come back and they will. Treat them as if you are doing them a favor by being there, and they will go elsewhere. You can count on it.

# The Bad Location

There is an old adage that when you are thinking of opening a new business, think: *location, location, location*. That says it all. If you start a business in the wrong location, you are just destined to go out-of-business.

In a small town the best location for a retail store front is on its main street. A side street business (off of the main street) can be a real business killer. The next time you are in a tourist town, watch the flow of foot traffic. Everyone is walking up and down the main boulevard, but very few people make a turn to walk down a side street.

The second part of a great *location* is parking. You need the ability for automobile traffic to stop and park to create foot traffic. This is what a mall parking lot is all about. Customers can drive from home to the mall, park their car and become the foot traffic (walking the mall) the mall businesses need.

A retail store of any kind that is located on a busy street with cars zooming along, and only a few parking spots out front, will never get the foot traffic of a mall.

Sometimes, however, even a strip mall (small mall on a main boulevard with a few dozen parking spaces) is no guarantee of success, especially if others have opened businesses there and have failed.

Case in point: There was the mini-market that had gone out-of-business because the strip mall just did not attract enough foot traffic to keep the business going. The sad part here was that someone else came along and felt that he could re-open the mini-mart and make it a success. Do I need to tell you what happened here? He also failed.

This was no surprise because it came back to *location, location, location*. While it was a busy street, the surrounding area had homes, not apartments. Just down the street from the mini-mart were two full size grocery stores. No one was going to the first mini-mart (that went out-of-business). So why would people go to the mini-mart when someone else re-opens it. The answer is: *they didn't*.

The lesson learned here is simple. If other businesses have gone out-of-business at some location, don't think you will be successful in the same spot with the same type of business. While a mini-mart may fail, an auto parts in the same location might do very well. Sometimes one type of business can succeed, while another type in the same location will fail.

# The Client List

When you start a small business, the underlining objective should be to sell it someday for a nice profit or even a nice retirement. The number one reason someone will buy an already established business is because of the clientele that already patronize the establishment. Think of it this way. If money was not an object, would you want to set-up a new hardware store and hope that people will come to it, or buy an existing Ace Hardware franchise?

The concept here is simple. You want a business that people will frequent and has a good reputation. The name, Ace Hardware, alone will attract customers.

When the day comes for you to sell your business, you will not only be selling the business reputation in the community, but more importantly, you will be selling your client list. This is the list of the names and addresses of all your clients with whom you have been doing business all these years. It includes the clients to whom you have been sending out monthly mailers and discount information, the contact information of the clients that made big purchases (the ones that took months of *prospecting* to get) and the list of companies that make seasonal purchases. That list is the life blood of your company and it is worth a great deal.

Years ago, as a business broker, I sold a manufacturing company. The original owner did all of the *prospecting*, made the *presentation* and went for the *close*. The new owner lacked all of these three skills and hired a salesperson to do the selling for him. Upon doing a follow-up of the business sale with the new owner a few months later, I had the opportunity to meet his new salesperson. This person knew sales and was good at *prospecting, presentation,* and *close*. When the new owner told me that he had printed out and given the new salesperson his whole company's list of clients for her to call on, I almost fell out of my chair. This new owner had paid over $250,000 for this business and just *gave away* 16 years of client history to a new salesperson. If I ever had to make up a list of the most absolute stupid, dumbest and idiotic things an owner could do, that would be right at the top of my list.

Because of the new owner's lack of (just about everything it takes to run a business) leadership and communication skills, his new salesperson only worked for him for one month. Would you like to guess where she went next? You're right. She went straight to his number one competitor, taking with her his whole client list. I happened to stop in some time later to see that competitor. He had just signed a contract with a client that had belonged to the other company. How did he get the name, phone number and detailed information of what that client needed? Of course, he got it from the client list that the new owner handed over to his sales agent. That, as unbelievable as it may sound, is a true story.

Obviously, this owner of the business ended up going out-of-business. Someone else stepped in and purchased the business at a very low price. Then with a lot of hard work the new owner brought the business back up by using the principles of *prospecting, presentation,* and *close.*

The lesson learned here is simple. Your client list *is* the heart and worth of your company. Never give it to anyone. If you hire a salesperson, you need to tell that person that it is his or her job to go out and find new business. There is no need for you to give anyone your client list as you already have those persons and companies as your clients. That is proprietary information. It should be guarded and never given away.

# The Customer is Always *Right* and Don't Forget It.

At some point in your business life, you will get the *customer from hell.* Every business owner has one (or more), and many times they remain your customers. They just keep coming back even if you wish they would just go away (to your competition).

The bottom line, however, is that no matter what happens or what they say, *"the customer is always right."* And you have to find the way to *smooth over the situation.*

A dissatisfied customer will tell everyone he or she knows what a bad business you have or how inferior your product or service is. Many of these people have other problems with life in general, which is an even a bigger reason for you to try and *smooth* out the situation and make things right for him or her. Don't get on the *defensive wagon.* Try your best to work it out and move on (in your life and business).

* * *

There are so many stories about business owners who make really bad business decisions. One way to avoid becoming a *statistic* is to take your time and really think out your new plan. Talk to other business owners, or go on-line and see if you can find information on what you are about to do. Check whether there are any comments others have written that may help you. Remember, it might be a new idea to you, but in business, someone else, someplace at sometime has most likely tried the same thing or something close to it.

And please don't think that paying another company to handle your advertising is going to save you time and bring in all this new business. It most likely will not. All you are doing is handing over your money to another company.

Learn how to *prospect* for new clients constantly, that is, every hour, everyday, and every week. Practice your *presentation* over and over until you can give it without stumbling all over your words. Then learn how to *close* the deal.

Every company must have great products or product lines, that is a given. How good you are at finding customers will not do you any good if your product or service is inferior. Many companies have great products to sell or services to provide. If, however, you want to know what makes some companies superior and stand out from the rest, you will find that it comes down to their outstanding ability to implement the techniques of *prospecting, presentation,* and *close.* You will find that they are experts in each of these areas.

On the following page there is a *Prospecting Punch List.* Review it and try your best to implement as many as you can each day. If you do, success could be right around the corner.

# *Prospecting Punch List*

In an effort to help you *kick-start* your *prospecting* efforts, here is a list of potential ways to find new clients. Depending on your type of business, you will need to determine what will work for you. I would, however, suggest that you try all of them and then focus on the ones that work the best.

1. Mix, mingle, meet and greet as many people as you can each and every day. Talk to the people in line with you at the bank, grocery store, post office, and fast food/take-out line. Anytime there are people near you, talk to them and talk about your business. No one is going to say: *"Oh shut up."* But someone might just be looking for what you have to offer or may know someone else that could use your product or service.

2. Remember to pass out at least six business cards each day. Review Chapter 4.

3. Keep a stack of fliers about your company in your car at all times. When you see a potential prospect, hand one to him or her.

4. Every major newspaper (those that are left) publish annual reports of the top 100 (500 or 1000) businesses in its city. This list contains each company's

name, address and telephone number. Many times it lists the names of the CEO right down to the VP of marketing. I have even seen purchasing agents listed. Get your hands of one of these reports and start making your calls. Many newspapers also put out a "top 40 under 40" (40 people under the age of 40 that are successful in your town) or something similar. This is another great tool for getting names of people who may need your product or services.

5. Make it a habit each morning to catch up on the local news especially business and local events. You will be amazed at the businesses and contact names that are mentioned. If you think they could use your products or services, give them a call.

6. Join your local chamber of commerce. When you do, its representative will hand you a list of all its members. Start calling. (Review Chapter 4) Attend the chamber of commerce functions, especially the monthly mixers. Take a stack of business cards and some fliers with you and walk around to everyone you see. Introduce yourself, your company and your products/services to each person you meet.

7. Get involved in your community. Volunteer for a fund raising event or a soup kitchen during the holidays. Help out and make sure you have someone take a picture of you when you are there. Then submit the photo to your local newspaper. Local newspapers are always looking for news on what its readers are doing for the community. This helps get you and your company's name out there.

8. Volunteer once a month to go out and pick up trash along the highway. Again, have a photo taken and submit it to the local paper. The goal here is to make your community aware of who you are and what your company is about.

9. Get involved in your industry by attending its conventions. This is a great way to network with those in the same industry. Many times you will make contacts with people who may refer you and your company to others for a job they don't want to take on. Subscribe to magazines for your industry and stay on top of trends.

10. Follow up after every sale. Your purchaser may have friends who want or need your product or service. And don't forget to send everyone on your list a card or newsletter (or something) in the month of January, not December. Tell them you look forward to another year and thank them for making your last year a success.

11. Stay physically and mentally fit. Your business will be of no value to anyone if you can't run it. Don't let hard times in business bring you down. Have fun each and every day. (Are we having fun yet?) Learn how to pace yourself so you aren't a victim of burn-out.

12. Remember, the next person you meet may need what you have to sell. So talk to them and listen to what they say. Review *Needs Satisfaction Selling* (Chapter 8).

"If you have built castles in the air, your work need not be lost; that is where they should be. Now put the foundations under them."

Henry David Thoreau
*1817 - 1862*

# Conclusion

If you have read this whole book, you should have a pretty good idea of what it is going to take to put *prospecting, presentation,* and *close* to work for you. The big question, of course, is: *"Can you do it?"* The answer has to be *"YES."* Don't even try to go into business if you feel you cannot learn to master each of those processes (or hire others to do it for you) or you will fail.

For those of you who are just interested in being a sales person, there is one other option. Go to work for someone else and specialize in *prospecting* for new clients. Then, turn your prospects over to the sales department. Let them make the *presentation* and *close* the sale. Believe it or not, but there are many large organizations that have very large departments that just focus on finding prospective buyers for their products or services.

If *prospecting* is not for you, perhaps you can focus on the *presentation* side. If you are comfortable standing up in front of people and giving a *presentation,* become a *presentation* specialist. Think of the times you may have gone to some meeting, and one person stood up and made a *presentation.* After the *presentation,* a different group of salespeople came in to go for the *close*. Someone has to make the *presentation*, so why not you?

Of course, there is the ultimate going for the *close* or making the sale. When everything else is said and done, without sales there will be no income for the company. It is the sales people who keep everything in this country moving forward. Manufacturers make the goods; truckers, trains and airplanes move them across country. Warehouses house the goods, distributors distribute, and retail stores sell them. But the key word is *sell.* If sales people do not sell the goods, everything starts to back up and eventually nothing moves.

If you are going to go for the American dream of owning your own business and becoming your own boss, you must master *prospecting, presentation,* and *close,* along with everything else that is involved with running a business. Please don't think that owning a small business and running an advertisement in the local yellow page directory will make you successful, because it will not. Yellow page advertizing is just one phase of your marketing program. Whatever you do, do not run a large display advertisement unless you sell and deliver pizza. For all other types of businesses, yellow page advertising is not going to bring you that much business. In fact, ask yourself this question: *"When was the last time you looked for a business (other than pizza) in the yellow pages?"* If you are not using it, what makes you thinks others will use it to find your business?

Finally, before you spend money buying equipment, renting a store front and fixing up the store, make sure you know how to sell your product or service. If you do not know how to *prospect* for new clients, give a persuasive *presentation* as to why they should buy from you and then go for the *close* (sale), you will be on the road to business failure, not success. You must master *prospecting, presentation,* and *close.* Your small business survival depends on it. Learn how to do all three and success for you, as a sales person or as a business owner, will be right around the corner.

*Now, go for it and make it happen!*

Jerry X Shea

# *About the Author*

Jerry X Shea has spent his whole life involved in selling products or services for his companies including a coffee/espresso shop, real estate office (where he specialized in small business opportunity sales), screen printing/embroidery company, impulse items distribution company, film production company, and as a wedding/baby photographer (his first business when he was in his '20s).

He is an accomplished keynote speaker and lecturer to the small business community through small business workshops, chambers of commerce events and various business related conferences and conventions. His first book, *IT LOOKS EASY! IS IT? Simple Steps for Small Business Success* (ISBN 0-9712622-0-9), is a must read for anyone going into business.

Mr. Shea's workshops on *Prospecting - Presentation - Close* fill the rooms at business conventions. His business magazine articles on the same subject have been re-printed many times.

Mr. Shea presents an exceptional outlook into life's experiences as they pertain to dealing with people (in business) and setting goals for oneself. He understands the daily struggles many small business owners face and draws upon his own personal insights and experiences to help other small business owners succeed in their businesses.

Mr. Shea is a firm believer that *salespeople turn the world* and that being a salesperson is indeed a noble profession.

# <u>*Notes*</u>